Bunratty Castle

THE CASTLES OF
NORTH MUNSTER

Mike Salter

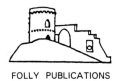

FOLLY PUBLICATIONS

ACKNOWLEDGEMENTS

The illustrations in this book are mostly the product of the author's own site surveys since 1971. Plans redrawn from his field note books are mostly reproduced to scales of 1:400 for keeps, tower houses, stronghouses and gatehouses, and 1:800 for courtyard castles and bawns, whilst large bawns and earthworks are shown at 1:2000. Jeremy Morfey took the photo of Ballynakill on page 112 and drove on one field trip in 2003, whilst Ian Rennie drove on another trip in 2003. Max Barfield took the photos of Limerick on page 6 and Ballinalacken on page 18 and drove on a 1992 trip. Helen Thomas drove on a trip in 2004 and checked parts of the text. Thanks are due to all of them, and to Ken McLeod and staff at Ennis Library for providing information, and to the staff of the Bodleian Library at Oxford, especially the map section. Finally, much advice and information was provided by Eamon Cody and several other members of staff at the National Monuments Section of the Department of the Environment, Heritage and Local Government in Dublin. A few of the plans are at least partly based on notes or drawings in their archaeological records.

AUTHOR'S NOTES

This book is the fifth and final volume of a new series superseding the author's previous work Castles and Stronghouses of Ireland, published in 1993 and now out of print. It is part of a series of books about castles throughout the British Isles all in a similar style with plans on a set of common metric scales allowing useful comparisons of sizes, wall thicknesses, etc. It is recommended that visitors use the Ordnance Survey 1:50,000 scale maps to locate the monuments, and grid references are given in the gazetteers. The books are intended as portable field guides giving as much information and illustrative material as possible in a book of modest size, weight and price, especially providing material about buildings not properly described elsewhere in print. The aim has been to give some basic information about owners or custodians of castles but no attempt has been made to provide detailed family genealogical histories. Ghost stories, myths and legends are not normally included, and personalities later than the 1690s are generally only mentioned if of relevant to the subsequent structural development or current condition of buildings.

All dimensions are given in metres and usually refer to the external size of a building at or near ground level, but above the plinth if there is one. Most towers and hall-houses will be smaller than the quoted dimensions higher up because of the external batter of the walls. Nearly all of the measurements quoted were personally taken on site by the author. On plans the original work is shown black, post-1800 work is shown stippled, and alterations and additions of intermediate periods are shown hatched. Each level is called a storey, sleeping and storage lofts tucked under vaults being usually treated as full storeys, and the basement being the first or lowest storey with its floor at or near ground level unless mentioned as otherwise. An attic room entirely within the height of a gabled roof is usually mentioned as an extra level additional to the number of storeys given.

ABOUT THE AUTHOR

Mike Salter is 50 and has been a professional author and publisher since 1988. He is particularly interested in the planning and layout of medieval buildings and has a huge collection of plans of castles and churches he has measured during tours (mostly by bicycle and motorcycle) throughout all parts of the British Isles since 1968. Wolverhampton born and bred, Mike now lives in an old cottage beside the Malvern Hills. His other interests include walking, maps, railways, board games, morris dancing and playing percussion instruments and calling folk dances with an occasional folk group.

First published December 2004. Copyright 2004 Mike Salter.
Folly Publications, Folly Cottage, 151 West Malvern Rd, Malvern, Worcs WR14 4AY
Printed by Aspect Design, 89 Newtown Rd, Malvern, Worcestershire WR14 2PD

Kilcash Castle, Tipperary

CONTENTS

Maps of extant castles appear inside the front and back covers.

BRIEF HISTORICAL INTRODUCTION

Not long before the Normans arrived in Ireland in 1169 Munster had been divided into two kingdoms, Thomond or North Munster being ruled by the O'Briens. The invading Normans soon took over much of what later became the counties of Limerick and Tipperary, whilst the O'Briens remained in control of the poorer lands of Clare. The Normans were able to exploit the Gaelic system of tanistry or choosing an heir from any of a chief's male relatives, which led to much infighting amongst the clans. Theobald Walter took most of Tipperary and established his main seat at Nenagh. His descendants took the surname Butler from Theobald's office of royal butler. In 1316 Edmund Butler was created Earl of Carrick by King Edward II of England, and in 1328 his successor James was given an additional earldom of Ormond by King Edward III. Most of Limerick was taken by Maurice FitzGerald, who also took most of Kerry and parts of Cork in South Munster. From him were descended two branches of the FitzGerald family. One became earls of Desmond, originally based at Shanid in Limerick, but later with their main seat at Tralee in Kerry, although they had other important castles in Limerick at Askeaton and Newcastle West. The other branch were created earls of Kildare and mostly held estates in Leinster, although they also held an important estate in Limerick centred on a castle at Adare.

The creation of the new earldoms was an unsuccessful attempt by the English crown to retain influence in Ireland. The Gaelic-speaking Irish remained in the majority and during the 14th century they gradually took back lands lost to the Normans in the 12th and 13th centuries. By the late 15th century the English crown had little influence in Ireland outside of a small area known as The Pale around Dublin. The Anglo-Norman lords became increasingly independent and some of them, especially the Desmond FitzGeralds, adopted Gaelic speech and customs. The earls of Ormond maintained at least a nominal allegiance to the crown, although they had abandoned Nenagh in the face of a Gaelic resurgence in the late 14th century and established a new power base further east at Kilkenny in Leinster. Tipperary had several walled towns where the English language, law and customs prevailed, but Limerick had only two walled towns, Limerick itself and Kilmallock, and there were none in Clare, where the O'Briens and MacNamaras remained all-powerful.

Killagh Castle, Tipperary

Urban tower house at Limerick

Arcaded curtain wall, Newcastle, Tipperary

In the 16th century the English crown managed to recover its influence in Ireland. It broke the power of the Kildare FitzGeralds in the 1530s, and that of the Desmond FitzGeralds in the 1580s, the earl being captured and executed in 1583 after being in rebellion since 1579. The lands of the Desmond FitzGeralds and their supporters were confiscated and given to Protestant English settlers. The Reformation of the church in the 1530s and 40s further complicated loyalties and allegiances in Ireland. The Gaelic Irish mostly remained Catholic, as did some of the Anglo-Norman families. The earls of Ormond and most of the inhabitants of the walled towns became Protestant. Clare remained most Catholic although some of the O'Briens became Protestant after their chief submitted to the English crown, accepting Protestantism and the title earl of Thomond.

Murrough O'Brien, Lord Inchiquin was one of the leaders of the loyal (or Parliamentary) forces in Munster during the wars of the 1640s against the rebel Confederate Catholics (who were, in effect, Royalists). Quite a number of castles played a part in this conflict, as did the city of Limerick. The final blow to the Gaelic Catholic cause was Cromwell's invasion of 1649 and the subsequent widespread confiscation of lands in the mid 1650s which were all handed over to Protestants, many of the settlers being former officers of Cromwell's army. There were, however, instances of where the original families remained on the lands (and in some cases still in occupation of the local castle) as tenants of the new landlords, who were sometimes absentees. In the 1690s there was another round of confiscations of lands belonging to supporters of the defeated and exiled James II. The city of Limerick again played a major part in the campaign of 1689-91.

Although sometimes able to withstand infantry attacks during the wars of the 16th and 17th centuries, the Irish tower houses were unable to resist cannonfire and were usually quickly surrendered when bombarded. Although available to the Lord Deputy appointed by the Crown, cannon do not seem to have been widespread in Ireland during the 16th century except in government forts and town defences. There is little evidence of them being deployed at the seats of the great lords except in times of war, and none of the castles in North Munster contain gunports suitable for firing heavy cannon out of. Cannon large enough to smash castle walls were very expensive and few landowners could have afforded them, although by the late 16th century muskets and pistols were common enough and castles of that period are equipped with small loops suitable for the discharge of these weapons. Equipped with a modern and efficient train of siege-artillery, Cromwell was quickly able to reduce all castles that offered resistance during his campaigns of 1649-50. That heralded the end of castles in all parts of the British Isles functioning as private owned defensible residences. Forts of later periods were state-run institutions with a purely military purpose built for the benefit of the country as a whole. By the 18th century most of the Irish castles not burnt or blown up during or after the wars of 1640-52 and 1689-91 had been abandoned in favour of more modern country houses.

ARCHITECTURAL INTRODUCTION

Forts built either of limestone blocks laid without mortar or with earth ramparts surmounted by a hedge or palisade and fronted by a ditch were common in Ireland during the Dark Ages, although most of the many ringforts were simply farmsteads rather than fortresses. Although there is some evidence of the Irish building castles and beginning to adopt the feudal system of land tenure by the early 12th century, it was the Norman invasion of the late 12th century that resulted in the widescale introduction of castles and feudalism within Ireland. Only a few major castles initially had stone buildings and the majority of the late 12th century castles took the form of a timber house or tower within a small palisaded court set upon a motte, a wholly or partly man-made flat-topped mound raised from material taken out of a surrounding ditch. Sometimes there was an accompanying enclosure or bailey containing wooden buildings and defended by a palisade on an earth rampart with a ditch in front. Alternatively the mound might take a larger but lower form known as a ringwork and combine the functions of both motte and bailey. In some cases natural features such as drumlins or promontories were adapted to form castles of the motte or ringwork types. These castles vary considerably in size and strength according to the needs and resources of those that built them, but few have mounds or ramparts higher than 8m. Most ringworks are between 20m and 35m across on top, whilst Irish mottes rarely have summits more than 15m across. Some of these sites are quite modest in size and the majority are now overgrown, sometimes to the point where little can be seen of the earthworks. This book is essentially about stone castles, and, since few of the mottes and ringworks have been properly surveyed or excavated, most of them are here merely listed. The only earthworks described in the gazetteers and their supplementary lists are those which had stone defences, plus the odd one or two that have been excavated, and a few whose construction by the Normans or destruction by the Irish is recorded by contemporary chroniclers.

Most of the earthwork castle sites of North Munster occur in Limerick and Tipperary and these counties also contain a number of manor-house sites taking the form of a square or rectangular platform 30m or 40m across surrounded by remains of a water-filled moat. Such moats provided some protection against malefactors and wild animals and also provided enclosures to safely secure domestic animals. They also served as status symbols, since they could only be built by landowners or their chief tenants.

Limerick Castle

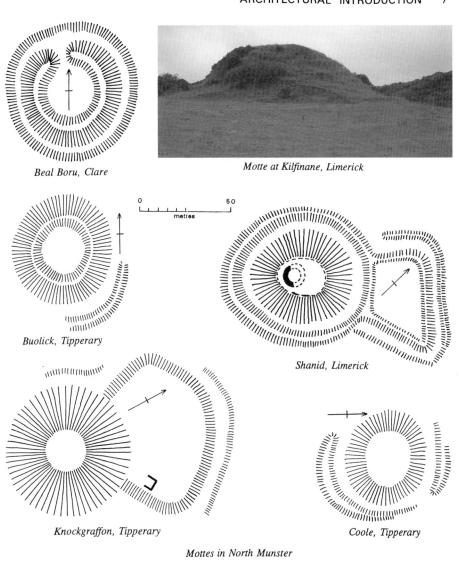

Beal Boru, Clare

Motte at Kilfinane, Limerick

Buolick, Tipperary

Shanid, Limerick

Knockgraffon, Tipperary

Coole, Tipperary

Mottes in North Munster

There are quite a number of castles in Limerick and Tipperary with important remains of the period 1200-20. Of a royal castle at Limerick with stone curtain walls around a nearly square court there remain about half of the walls, plus three circular corner towers and a gatehouse with two circular towers flanking the entrance passage, which was closed by a portcullis. Theobald Walter's castle at Nenagh also had a gatehouse of this type and circular towers around a small court which was more circular in plan. Here the principal surviving part is a huge circular tower keep, considerably larger and more massive than the other towers. Two other circular keeps in Tipperary lying at the corners of much-altered courtyards at Ardfinnan and Kiltinan are probably of later in the 13th century but in County Limerick there is a fragment of a keep of c1200 which was polygonal externally but circular internally perched upon a motte at the FitzGerald seat of Shanid.

Sheela-na-gig at Farney

Adare Castle, Limerick

Part of the stone wall upon the ringwork at Adare, together with one open-backed D-shaped tower and a hall-block outside the ringwork, are also thought to be of c1200. Later in the 13th century a wall with a square gatehouse was built to link the inner ward with the hall, a square tower keep was built within the inner ward, and a spacious new aisled hall with a porch and service rooms was built east of the older hall. Rather more altered 13th century halls also remain in the Limerick castles of Askeaton and Carrigogunnell, whilst Newcastle West has a 15th century hall converted from a 13th century chapel.

Limerick contains two substantial hall keeps of c1200 both with clasping corner turrets and a larger turret centrally placed at one end to contain a wide spiral staircase. Only the lowest level remains at Castletown Conyers, but Castletown Coonagh is a spectacular ruin, half of it standing over 20m high. There are slightly later hall-keeps at Newcastle and Templemore in Tipperary with remains of walled courts, the curtain at Newcastle being arcaded internally. Kilfinny and Tomdeeley in County Limerick are thinly walled hall houses long enough contain a public hall and private chamber end to end. A dozen other hall houses in Tipperary all have thicker walls with battered bases and compare with many others found in Galway, Mayo, and Sligo. Most of them have suffered quite a lot of alteration with vaults and larger new windows often being inserted during the 15th and 16th centuries. The hall houses at Drummeen and Dangan Iviggin in Clare may be 14th century. Rarer in other parts of Ireland, hall-houses were mostly built by knights serving the main Norman lords, although Tomdeeley was a seat of the bishop of Limerick. The lesser status of the Limerick and Tipperary hall-houses is indicated by a lack of enclosing stone walls, although each hall-house presumably once had a ditch and palisade to enclose the accompanying wooden buildings. Each contained a single large chamber, usually with a latrine and lancet windows set in embrasures with seats, and set over a dark basement used for storage. Commonly each level would have its own separate entrance.

Tomdeeley Castle, Limerick

Nenagh: plan of keep

In the 1270s and 80s Thomas de Clare built a number of stone castles as part of a campaign against the O'Briens. Castle Connell in Limerick may have been one of them and is said to have had two circular corner towers. Not much remains of it or of several others in the southern part of County Clare, all of which were soon over-run by the O'Briens and destroyed. One tower of a twin-towered gatehouse remains at Clare Castle, and the bases of three circular corner towers and the walls connecting them at Quin. This building probably had a tiny central court surrounded by three or four ranges of timber-framed buildings set against the curtain walls, an arrangement similar to the layout of the better preserved building at Ferns in Co Wexford. The de Birmingham stronghold of Castle Grace in Tipperary, where two circular towers and a wall linking them remain, was a slightly more spacious castle of this type, and one tower remains of another at Brittas. Another building with four circular corner towers, but with a solid central body instead of with ranges around a court, was begun by the Butlers sometime during the 13th century at Old Court, Terryglass, in Tipperary. The best preserved late 13th century stronghold in North Munster, however, is the castle which King Edward I built at Roscrea in the 1280s. Three quarters of the curtain wall of the D-shaped court remains, together with two D-shaped towers and a recently restored rectangular gatehouse. This gatehouse was later remodelled into a tower house and a new gateway made alongside, as also happened in another late 13th century castle at Cahir, which has a square court with two square corner towers, although much of the building as it now stands is the product of later medieval remodelling and a mid 19th century restoration.

Secular buildings which can be dated with certainty to the 14th century are not common in Ireland. A few of the tower houses about to be discussed could be of c1370-1400 and represent a development from hall-houses, two of which are probably 14th century anyway, as are a chapel at Newcastle West, and a building with a circular corner tower at Tullow, and a keep and bawn at Clonamicklon, both in Tipperary. Of c1400 is the castle at Glenogra in Limerick, unique in having a square court with one octagonal corner tower standing complete and the lower part of another. Its closest relative amongst British castles is that begun c1380 by the Stafford family at Newport in South Wales.

Keep at Nenagh, Tipperary

Gateway at Roscrea, Tipperary

Lisnacullia Castle, Limerick

Oola Castle, Limerick

Nearly all of the castles built in Ireland during the 15th and 16th centuries were of the type now known as a tower house and contemporaries simply referred to them as castles. Tower houses are common also in Scotland and the northern parts of England, They seem to have been generally regarded as a suitable form of residence for landowners requiring a tall embattled building as a status symbol and refuge in strife-torn areas where raiding was endemic and attempts by the government to maintain the peace were only sporadic or non-existent. For the defence of The Pale around Dublin in Leinster Henry VI's Irish government encouraged the erection of building small towers by offering a cash subsidy for their construction. It is doubtful if this had much effect on what went on in Munster. It seems that the earls of Desmond and Ormond and their relatives and chief tenants, plus powerful Gaelic chiefs such as the MacNamaras, had built impressive new tower houses by the mid 15th century and that others later followed their example. The towers vary in size and massiveness depending on the status and wealth of the person the tower was originally meant to accommodate, or the importance attached to defending a place of strategic importance such as a river crossing or mountain pass. Sometimes there was a need to impress local inhabitants after an estate or district changed hands, whether by marriage, purchase, inheritance, a grant or exchange of lands, or military conquest.

Of about 440 castellated buildings dating from c1200 to c1650 of which there are still standing remains in Clare, Limerick, and Tipperary, about 330 of them were tower houses dating from the second half of that period. Sixteen tower houses are still inhabited, some of them in a much modified or cut-down form, and a few others are roofed but not occupied as dwellings. All the rest are ruins ranging from almost complete shells to minor fragments or footings buried under piles of fallen debris. Most towers now stand alone in the fields, although they were usually originally accompanied by outbuildings such as barns, and sometimes had gardens and orchards alongside them. A few lie next to later houses or farm buildings, but in some cases these later buildings are also now ruinous.

Bawn at Nicholastown, Tipperary

In Tipperary the towers of Ballynakill, Ballynahinch, Knockkelly, Moorstown and Moycarkey lie within rectangular walled bawns dating from c1550-1620. All these are fairly spacious, have wall-walks with gunloops in the parapets, and the last three have two circular turrets known as flankers (with gunloops on two levels) at diagonally opposite corners, a layout also found in the smaller bawn around the tower at Ballyportree in Clare, whilst Garraunboy in Limerick had a bawn with four flankers. The pair of bawns side-by-side at Ballygrennan in Limerick have bartizans but no flankers and may be as late as c1625-50. Cappagh is another Limerick tower with inner and outer bawns. Another two dozen towers in North Munster have fragmentary bawns mostly of modest size, and there are some examples of bawns where no tower existed or has survived, as at Ballyculhane in Limerick, which has four square corner turrets. Several more ruinous bawns in the Burren of County Clare may have been of drystone construction and were livestock enclosures rather than defences. Bawns with thin walls with a coped top instead of a wall-walk and parapet, as at Nicholastown in Tipperary, also were of minimal defensive value unless provided with gunloops at ground level, as at Kilconnell. The bawn gateways were usually just a simple arch in the wall, although sometimes surmounted by a machicolation. Only at Moorstown (and, as additions, at two older drystone cashels in the Burren) was there a proper gatehouse. The gateways were closed by two-leaved doors secured with drawbars, neither the bawns or their towers usually being fitted with portcullises.

Bawn gateway, Ballinalacken

Borrisoleigh Castle

Two views of Moyneard Castle, Tipperary

There are enough variations in the planning and features of the tower houses of North Munster to make them interesting, but some arrangements and features are very common indeed. There are eighteen circular tower houses, all of the 16th century and mostly in Tipperary and the Burren of Clare, but the majority of the tower houses are rectangular. Most of them do not have any projections at ground level, although about twenty examples have a small projecting turret to contain latrines or a wing to provide extra private rooms. Many of the towers have a graceful batter throughout their height but some are battered in their lower parts only and then rise vertically.

Many of the towers in Clare and Limerick have at one end a spiral staircase adjoining a tier of lesser chambers with a murder-hole in the floor of the lowest covering the entrance passage below. There are a number of examples where vertical joints indicate that this end of the tower was built first and the main part added later. Carrigaholt and Cratloekeel in Clare, and Tullovin in Limerick are examples of where only the mural chambers and stair were ever built, the main body of the tower never having been added as intended. At Leamaneh the building eventually added to the tier of chambers was a fortified house rather longer than the main body of the tower originally intended. Many of the towers on the Butler lands in Tipperary have a rather different layout following the design of other Butler towers in Co Kilkenny. These towers often have an entrance in a long wall and access to the upper parts by means of long straight flights of steps, although sometimes an end wall higher up is thickened to contain a tier of lesser chambers.

Two views of Fethard, Tipperary

The entrance doorway of a tower house was usually covered by an external machicolation from the wall-walk and closed by a wooden door opening inwards and secured by a drawbar. Some towers also had the jambs recessed externally to provide for a hinged iron grille called a yett which opened outwards and was secured by a chain passing through a hole (looking like a gunloop) in one jamb. This arrangement probably would have allowed a tower to be left empty and secured by padlocking the yett from the outside, in total contrast to the yetts of Scottish and Northumbrian towers which open inwards and needed someone left inside the tower to secure it.

Many of the tower houses had four storeys, although some of the Tipperary towers had five storeys. In this book each level is called a storey, even if it was no more than a storage loft or sleeping attic lighted by a single loop in an end wall and squeezed under a stone vault. Many of the towers have a vault below the topmost room, but sometimes there was a second vault at a lower level. Some large and massive 15th century towers in Clare had just three lofty storeys with vaults over the lowest two. Vaults may be semi-circular, segmental or pointed in section, and where there are two they may be of different forms. Unlike the 13th and 14th century plank-centred vaults, 15th and 16th century vaults in Ireland were usually formed over mats of wickerwork laid on timber frames and often show signs of these mats, which were often left in place and plastered over.

Sometimes there are extra mural rooms in the other walls apart from those provided in a tier in a thick end wall. The haunches of vaults were sometimes left hollow, partly to lighten the load on the outer walls, but also to allow space for passages and extra rooms. Some chambers in the haunches of vaults were "secret rooms" only reached by concealed trapdoors in the floors of passages or window embrasures above them. A common arrangement is for two latrines at different levels to descend into a long single chute in one of the long walls. At Drumline and Rathlaheen in Clare and a few other towers a passage behind the tier of mural chambers was carried on an arch over one end of one of the intermediate level main rooms to allow access the width of the building from the spiral staircase to a latrine in the far wall. This meant that anyone in the tower could use the latrine rather than just the occupant of one room.

Urlanbeg: vault with marks of wicker mat

Ballysheeda Castle, Tipperary

Fireplace at Kilcash, Tipperary   *Bawn Flanker at Moycarkey, Tipperary*

Many parapets protecting the wall-walks were knocked off towers in the 17th century as a way of making them indefensible, but where parapets do survive the merlons are usually tall and double-stepped in the typical Irish manner. Bartizans with machicolations between corbels are set at diagonally opposite corners and are usually circular with double-stepped corbels in Tipperary, but are sometimes square with inverted pyramidal corbels in Clare and Limerick. The roofs might be of slabs, slates or thatch, and there were sometimes attic rooms lighted by small windows in end gables set within the parapet.

Windows in Irish towers tend to be narrow. On the upper levels the lights may be paired and on the topmost level they may be tall enough for a transom to be provided, but the individual lights still remain narrow. The iron stanchions used elsewhere in Europe were less common on Irish towers, although they were used in the 17th century fortified houses and in the windows of churches and monastic buildings. For the sake of brevity in the gazetteers only those windows with ogival heads, hoodmoulds or other decorative features such as carved or sunk spandrels beside ogival heads are mentioned specifically. Other windows not described will have square-headed (or occasionally round-headed) lights. Generally these tall narrow windows were provided with internal shutters rather than glass. Occasionally a stone hanging eye for mounting the upper pivot of a window shutter or door will have survived the wrenching out of the timberwork when the tower was no longer required for habitation or storage. A speciality of Irish tower houses, rarely found in their Scottish and English counterparts, is the provision of loops in the middle storeys that pierce the outer corners of the towers. The embrasures of main room upper windows occasionally have built-in seats. The rere-arches are often semi-circular or segmental, although lintels are often used, especially for narrower embrasures lower down and for the embrasures of loops lighting mural chambers and passageways.

All the arrangements and features of tower houses described so far can occur at any period from the 1420s to the 1630s. There are, however certain features that seem to have begun to be used more commonly from about the 1540s, and these help us to decide whether a tower is likely to be early or late during the two and a half centuries of tower houses being in fashion in Ireland. None of the castles contain gunports for large cannon but many of the towers and the flankers of their bawns contain small round or square holes suitable for the discharge of muskets or pistols. Such weapons existed in Ireland by the 1490s but it is unlikely that Irish towers and bawns were equipped for systematic defence by firearms before the fall of the earls of Kildare in the 1530s. Gunloops are often found in bartizans and are sometimes placed on either side of windows or loops, opening off the same embrasure. A circular tower at Newtown in Clare has the rare but ingenious feature of gable-shaped recesses each commanded from the top by a gunloop in the sill of a window loop. Plain square-headed mullioned windows with lights wider than the tall ogival-headed late medieval type windows also became fashionable in the second half of the 16th century. There are examples of them in the tower at Newtown.

Ballynahinch Castle, Limerick

Cloondooan Castle

Towers with gunloops sometimes had wooden lintels instead of rere-arches over embrasures. They also tend to have fireplaces in their upper rooms and consequently there are chimney stacks at the top, those on sidewalls often partly or entirely impeding access round the wall-walk. Some late towers did not have full circuits of wall-walks and their roof gables rise directly off the outer wall-faces. At Danganbrack in Clare there were four gables and no wall-walks as such, although the corners had open bartizans. The evidence suggests that the lower and intermediate levels of 15th century towers in the west of Ireland were unheated but that where the topmost room lay over a vault (which was very common) it had a central hearth or brazier with a louvre in the roof to allow smoke to escape. This top room, by far the largest because of the internal thinning of the walls above the vault, was usually the main hall, the owner's private room being in one of the middle storeys of the building. This is the opposite of the usual English and Scottish preference for a public room directly over a vaulted cellar with more private rooms higher up. It may reflect the Gaelic landowners closer relationship with their followers, compared with the elitism and greater desire for privacy of the English lords. A few late towers such as Kilcash and Rathnaveoge in Tipperary have no vaults and buildings of this type may have had their main public room directly over the cellar, and bedrooms in the top levels.

There are a few instances of upper fireplaces (often with joggled or zig-zag jointed lintels and side brackets to help take the weight of the walling above) bearing initials of owners with dates, but these can be misleading as in some instances they refer to later alterations and not the original period of construction. Some 15th century towers were modernised in the period 1580-1640 by inserting fireplaces, large new windows and one or two gunloops. A tower at Rossroe which is probably one of the earliest in Clare had its cellar converted into a kitchen with a new fireplace. Clenagh, also in Clare, seems to have been later rebuilt from the third storey upwards. Here too the large fireplace in the lowest level appears to be an insertion. Rooms specifically designated and equipped as kitchens exist in the larger fortified houses, but kitchens (and also wells) are very rare in Irish tower houses. Chapels are also rare in tower houses, although there are two in corner turrets at Bunratty (which also has a kitchen) and a window embrasure facing NE in the L-shaped tower at Ballingarry in Limerick was obviously designed as an oratory.

Rineroe Castle

Fireplace at Ballinalacken

Carrick-on-Suir Castle

Bunratty is an exceptionally large 15th century tower house with the very unusual layout of four square corner towers which each contain five levels of private rooms opening off upper and lower halls over cellars. Other large 15th century buildings not of the standard tower house type are the apartment blocks added at Carrigogunnell and a three storey range at Askeaton with at one end a tier of private chambers with latrines in a side-turret. An older hall in the outer ward was also remodelled. Both these castles have 15th century bawn walls. Much of the castle at Cahir also dates from the 15th and 16th centuries, with the provision of a new inner gateway and the addition of a large new outer bawn. Carrick-on-Suir has a 15th century courtyard with two towers of equal importance facing to landward and remains of a third facing the river. Fethard has substantial remains of its later medieval town walls, in addition to two urban tower houses. Pairs of late medieval castellated buildings also remain at Thurles and Limerick, where the town walls are more fragmentary.

In the medieval period castle walls were often whitewashed both inside and out, thus making the best of the limited light admitted through the narrow windows. The lowest room (it was rarely subdivided in Irish tower houses) was generally used for storage. The living rooms above might sometimes have wall-paintings of biblical, allegorical, or heroic scenes or tapestries with similar motifs. Carpets were only introduced in the late 16th century, before which those floors not formed of planks laid on massive beams were made of rammed earth or clay. All the floors were covered with rushes changed periodically.

Inchicronan: plan

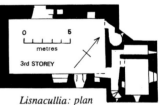

Lisnacullia: plan

Burncourt Castle

The sort of privacy we now all take for granted hardly existed in a medieval castle. Even nobles often had attendants sleeping in the same room or in a passage connecting the room to the main staircase, although the lordly bed would be screened off. Furniture was sparse and of the simplest and plainest kind until the 17th century. Only the owner and his immediate family were likely to have individual chairs, but the hall would contain tables and benches. Also suitable for seating were the chests within which clothes, plate and other valuables were kept. A notable feature of the towers is the number of lockers within the walls, nearly every window embrasure having one in some of the towers.

The defeat and forfeiture of the Earl of Desmond and his followers in 1580s led to a new plantation of parts of Munster with new Protestant settlers, some of whom preferred to dwell in new houses like the Elizabethan mansions of England with their spacious rooms filled with light from huge mullion-and-transom windows. Back in the 1560s the Earl of Ormond had added a two storey house of this type in front of the older castle at Carrick-on-Suir, its upper storey containing a rare Irish example of a long gallery. However the families settled on lands taken from the Desmond FitzGeralds mostly still felt a need to build houses retaining some defensive features such as gunloops and machicolations. About the same time some of the Gaelic Irish and Anglo-Norman families also began to build such houses. The four storey mansions with large windows at Leamaneh in Clare and Loughmoe in Tipperary were added to older towers and each has a projecting wing at the far end. There are quite a number of instances where a house was added to an older tower in the 17th century although in some cases little has survived other than a roof-mark left on the older building. Dating from the period immediately before the beginning of the wars of the 1640s are the houses of Burncourt and Killenure in Tipperary. Burncourt has four square tower towers each with four gables, whilst Killenure has circular corner towers, both being well provided with gunloops. The castles at Clarebeg and Clonamicklon in Tipperary looking like tower houses but with internal layout more like Elizabethan houses, although each make incorporate older work. Knockgraffon, also in Tipperary, has a stronghouse converted from the central part of a large medieval church in addition to a tower house and a motte and bailey site. The stronghouse at Roosca in Tipperary may go back to the early 16th century, since it had only narrow loops rather than wide windows. Ireton's Castle at Lehinch, dating from c1650 has at diagonally opposite corners a pair of pear-shaped towers with gunloops and single-storey triangular prows facing the field. This is probably the latest building of its type in North Munster. Other late 17th century houses in the province are thinly walled buildings without any defensive features.

ACCESS TO THE CASTLES

The following codes appear after the O.S. grid references in the gazetteers. They give only an indication since access arrangements may change from time to time, as may the amount of vegetation obscuring distant views, whilst some monuments may only be open during the summer months. Sites not given a code lie on private land and can only be seen by obtaining prior permission from the landowners. Only occasionally will a courteous request for access by those with a genuine interest in ancient buildings will be refused outright, although some owners may forbid visitors to enter ruins considered precarious. Visitors should in all cases close any gates that they need to open, ensure that their dogs do not cause any kind of nuisance to the farmers or their animals, and generally follow the maxim of taking away only photographs and leaving behind nothing but footprints.

A - Free access on foot to the whole site at any time. Mostly sites in state care.
B - Free access on foot at any time to the exterior only. Mostly sites in state care.
C - Private, but clearly visible from public road, path or other open space.
D - Private, but distant view usually possible from road, path or other open space.
E - Open to the public (fee usually payable) during certain hours (at least in summer).
G - Private, but fairly easy courtesy access is currently normally possible.
H - Buildings in use as hotels, shops, museums. Access to grounds usually possible.

CASTLES OF COUNTY CLARE

BALLINALACKEN   M104004   B

A high rock above a stream beside a hotel bears a well preserved ruined tower lying in a bawn 30m wide by 120m long which only required much of a wall towards the west where there is a round-arched gateway with corbels for a machicolation above. A straight joint indicates that the east end of the tower was built before the rest. This part has the entrance, with a machicolation high above, the staircase, and six levels of small rooms. The main block has two poorly lighted storeys under a vault, two better lighted storeys with windows of two and three lights above, and there was an attic within the wall-walk. Mid-wall box machicolations with gunloops open off the fourth storey, which has a fine fireplace dated 1644, when the castle was held by Daniel O'Brien. It was spared dismantling in 1654 since Daniel was a Protestant. The castle was granted to Captain Hamilton in 1667, although later recovered by Daniel's descendants.

BALLINTLEA   R488631

Not much remains of the west wall containing the entrance and staircase of this tower measuring 15m by 10m over walls 2.4m thick, but the eastern part stands about 14m high, showing evidence of three lofty storeys with vaults over the lowest two. The castle is said to have been built in the 15th century by Sioda, son of Philip Mor MacNamara, although it does not appear on the 1580 list. It was occupied until the late 19th century.

Ballyallia: plan

0   25
metres

3rd STOREY

1st STOREY

Ballinalacken Castle   Ballinalacken: plans & section

BALLYALLIA   R339815

English settlers in this castle were besieged for six weeks by the O'Briens in 1641. It was garrisoned by Cromwellian troops in the 1650s. Half buried in debris are the lower parts of the west, north and east walls of a tower about 10m by 7.4m and a fallen fragment.

BALLYCORICK   R280656

This O'Brien tower measures 9m by 9.6m with walls 1.8m thick except for one end wall 2.7m thick containing the entrance. The second storey is a vaulted loft with mural chambers in the north wall and SW corner. The NE corner has corbels for a room in a bartizan opening off the ruined third storey.

BALLYCULLEN   R503683   D

On an elevated plateau commanding a wide view to the west is a tower measuring 13.5m by 8.6m set in the SW corner of a bawn measuring 17m by 13m with circular flankers at the SE and NW corners. The flankers contain square vaulted rooms, that on the NW being set diagonally to the bawn. A third flanker has been added to the bawn NE corner. It lacks gunloops and may date from when a two storey range was inserted in the SE corner of the bawn in the 19th century to serve as a police barracks until c1920. The tower contains a cellar and a loft under a vault and one upper storey, although there was probably originally at least one further upper level. The north wall contains three levels of chambers over the entrance passage and guardroom and there is a damaged spiral stair in the NE corner. A low passage which had a wooden ceiling runs over an arch over the cellar to connect the spiral stair with a latrine in the west wall. The tower is thought to have been built in the 1430s by Donnchadh MacNamara and was captured in 1496 by the Earl of Kildare with the aid of artillery, although the locals later chased him away.

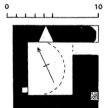

Ballycorick: plan

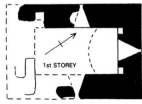

Ballintlea; plan

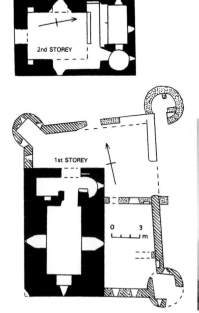

Plans of Ballycullen Castle

Ballycullen Castle

BALLYGRIFFY   R321830   C

This tower measuring 9m by 7.3m has an entrance below a tier of small rooms at the north end. A second doorway higher up, leading directly onto the foot of the spiral stair in the NE corner, communicated with a former east wing added later. This doorway is covered by gunloops in the treads of the stairs above. The lowest small room has a murder hole covering the other entrance. The top room of the tier is at the level of the wall-walk upon the four storey main block, which had an attic roof at this level.

BALLYHANNON or CASTLE FERGUS   R388726   D

This five storey tower with double-stepped battlements was restored in the 1970s. It has a tier of chambers over the east-facing entrance, which is covered by one of the machicolations set in the middle of each side. The spiral staircase in the SE corner has one of the two angle-loops at second storey level.

Ballymarkahan: plan

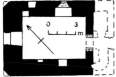

Ballynahinch: plan

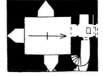

Ballygriffy: plan

Ballyshanny Castle

Ballymarkahan Castle

Ballynahinch Castle

BALLYMARKAHAN   R436729   D

Measuring 11.5m by 7.7m, this tower is said to have been built c1430 by Donall, son of Shane an Gabhaltais. The two walls 2.1m thick still standing above the foundations show that there were five storeys with vaults over the second and fourth. The 3.5m thick east wall contained a SE corner staircase and a tier of chambers. Passages carried on arches over the main rooms led from the staircase to latrines in the north wall at levels between the second and third storeys and the fourth and fifth storeys.

BALLYNAHINCH   R551806   D

The rock upon which this tower stands may have once been an island. Probably built c1475 by Donald MacNamara, the tower is 8m wide and was about 12.2m long when the SE wall containing the entrance and spiral staircase was more complete. The inner doorway remaining in this wall is a later rebuild. Little survives above the lofty vaulted basement. There was a latrine in the NE wall. In 1655 the castle was granted to Donnchadh O'Callaghan.

BALLYPORTRY   R300901   C

This is a five storey tower measuring 14m by 7.5m with pointed vaults over the first and fourth levels. The second and third storeys have fireplaces in the NW side wall and three-light windows in the SW end wall. At the top an arch is used to make this end wall thick enough to contain a chamber at wall-walk level. The other end contains five levels of chambers over the entrance passage and a spiral stair in the east corner. The sheela-na-gig in the stairwell dates only from the restoration by the American architect Bob Brown, by whom it was purchased in the 1960s. The tower is surrounded by a bawn 24m by 15m enclosed by a loopholed wall now about 2.7m high with circular east and west corner flankers, the former now re-roofed to make a conservatory. To the SW and SE are remains of an older and larger bawn. The castle was long held by a branch of the O'Briens who also held Leamanagh (see the entry for that castle). The castle was kept in repair by the O'Briens until they moved to Dromoland and was habitable throughout the 19th century.

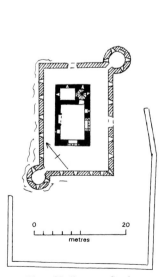

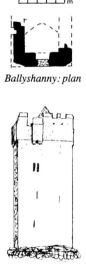

Ballyshanny: plan

Plan of Ballyportry Castle   *Ballyhannon Castle*

Ballyportry Castle

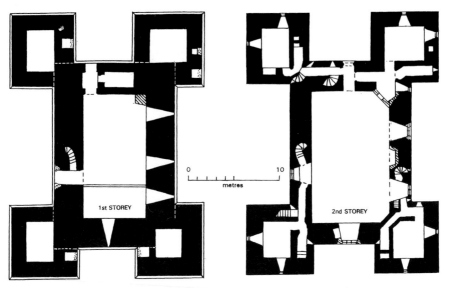

Plans of Bunratty Castle

BALLYSALLAGH or CASTLEKEEL   R379673   D

A fragmentary bawn about 48m square has a remains of a 17th century house measuring 32m by 8.4m on the east side and footings of a tower about 9m by 13m further west. Here in 1287 Thomas de Clare was killed in battle against Turlough O'Brien. In 1565 it was held by John McInenery of Kilkilty, although the MacClancys probably occupied it almost up until the time of the 1641 rebellion, when it was held by James Martin.

BALLYSHANNY   R187949   D

The east end remains of a tower 6.6m wide, the NE corner being four storeys high. Part the second storey vault remains. There is a latrine-chute on the south. The east wall has a triple-stepped corbel for what was probably a large third storey bartizan. See page 20.

BUNRATTY   R451609   E

After being granted Bunratty in 1277 Sir Thomas de Clare replaced the old earth and timber castle built by Robert de Muscegros with a new stone castle. It withstood attacks by the Irish in the 1290s but had been burnt by 1306. After Richard de Clare was routed and killed at Dysert O'Dea in 1318 his widow burnt the castle and sailed off to England. Supporters of the Earl of Desmond then seized Bunratty. Sir Thomas Rokeby refortified the site in 1353 but in 1355 it was captured and destroyed by Murchadh O'Brien.

The existing castle was in O'Brien hands from probably the late 15th century until 1712. After submitting to Henry VIII in 1543 Murrough O'Brien was created Earl of Thomond. Bunratty became a fine stately home noted for its ornamental grounds and park with three thousand deer. In 1645 Brian, 6th Earl handed the castle over to a Parliamentary force under Admiral William Penn, from whom it was captured by Lord Muskerry after a two month siege. The Stoddart family lived in the castle from the 1720s until in the early 19th century they transferred to a new house nearby. The castle was restored after its purchase by Lord Gort in 1954 and it now lies in the SE corner of a folk park of facsimile houses extending between it and the early 19th century mansion.

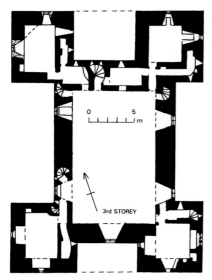

Bunratty Castle

Bunratty is the largest and most complex of Irish tower houses. Much of it could be the work of Maccon MacSioda MacNamara and his son Sean Finn c1445-70, embellished c1600-25, and with new parapets and roofs of the 1960s. However the main block lowest storey seems older and could represent Sir Thomas Rokeby's work of 1353, or could even go back to c1278-85. Above a battered base this lowest storey measures 19.4m by 13m over walls up to 3.3m thick and has its own entrance facing north. A stair leading up in the west wall looks as if it has been hacked through at a later date. The four corner turrets each about 7.2m square are bonded to the upper walls but are clearly additions to the lowest storey, except perhaps for the SE turret containing rooms cutting into the main block outer corner. This turret has a dungeon at ground level but the lowest habitable rooms in the other turrets are at the level of the vault over the main block lowest storey. This vault and that of a third storey mural room beside the main staircase in the 3.2m thick north wall have traces of plank centring, usually evidence of an early date.

A drawbridge leads to an upper entrance leading into the vaulted lower hall, where the three-light window at the south end and the east fireplace later insertions. Passages off the embrasures of two-light east and west windows give access to two levels of rooms in the southern turrets, the upper rooms being at the level of the hall vault. Rooms in the northern turrets are reached from the entrance passage and adjoining main staircase. This stair rises to the third storey main room, a lofty upper hall heated by a central hearth with a louvre in the roof. Passages and stairs from the upper hall northern corners and from the south sides of embrasures of two-light windows with transoms in the side-walls give access to the third, fourth and fifth habitable levels of the corner turrets plus solars at either end carried upon arches high up between the turrets. The north solar has a window towards the upper hall. The south solar, remodelled c1600-25 with a six-light window and a painted pendant ceiling, was reserved for important guests. The turret rooms all have a single-light window in each of the two sides away from the main block. Most of them have a latrine and several are vaulted. At upper hall level the NW turret contains a kitchen with a fine fireplace and the SE turret contains the main chapel, whilst the NE turret contains a private chapel higher up. The NE window embrasure of the upper hall contains a sheela-na-gig removed from one of the turret rooms. The two halls and the turret rooms contain Lord Gort's remarkable collection of imported furniture dating from c1400-1650.

Gateway at Cahermore

Caislean A'Mhagaidh

Carrahill: plan

Carrigaholt: plan

CAHERMACNAGHTEN   M197001   A

This fairly well-preserved ringfort about 30m in diameter has remains of a mortared late medieval gatehouse 4.8m wide projecting 3.7m within the older drystone outer wall. The fort was still in use in 1675 when there was a large house and kitchen and surrounding gardens. The inside ground level has gradually built up higher than that outside and has foundations of various structures. The O'Davorens ran a law school here.

CAHERMORE   M221044   A

This drystone fort has a mortared medieval gatehouse with a rebuilt lintelled portal leading to a passage flanked by small guard-rooms.

CAISLEAN A'MHAGAIDH   R179940   D

A very ruined wall 1.1m thick around a bawn 23m by 14m is best preserved on the NE, where a wing against the north wall extends east from a tower house base measuring about 11.6m by 9.4m.

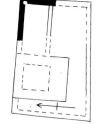

Caislean A'Mhagaidh

CAPPAGH   M321012

Nothing now remains of the east end of this O'Loughlan tower containing chambers over the entrance and the staircase. Parts of the later west end 6.8m wide remain, with part of a vault, a latrine-chute and a NW angle-loop, although much of it has fallen since 1900. The tower seems to have stood in the NW corner of a small bawn. It was captured by Cromwellian forces in c1652 and then granted to John Blake and John Morgan.

CARRAHILL   R394867

Remains of a building 7m wide and 15m long and a pile of debris from a possible tower house divide a court about 30m by 26m from a triangular outer court. Only footings face towards Inchicronan Lough but the vulnerable north wall of the outer court still stands 3.5m high and 1.4m thick with a gap marking a gateway, on either side of which are traces of buildings. Carrahill was held in 1641 by the Earl of Thomond.

Carrigaholt Castle

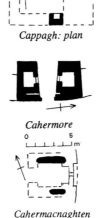

Cappagh: plan

Cahermore

0 5 m

Cahermacnaghten

Cappagh Castle

CARRIGAHOLT   Q849512   B

In the mid 16th century the MacMahon lords of Corcabascin built the 5m wide east wall of what was intended to be a large building 13m wide and probably over 15m long. The lack of a base batter and the presence of bonding stones lower down clearly indicate an intention to add a massively walled tower to the west. The ambitious scheme was abandoned and the east wall, which contains chambers on either side of a central entrance passage, plus a staircase in the southern part, was completed as a self-contained unit. The bawn may be 17th century, although it has a later gateway and the NE turret facing the pier is modern. Teige Caoch MacMahon was unsuccessfully besieged here by Sir Conyers Clifford in 1598, but a few months later the castle was captured by the Earl of Thomond after a four day siege. In breach of the surrender terms he hanged the garrison and handed the castle over to his brother Donal, who inserted several new windows and provided the fifth storey with a fireplace dated 1603 and a small room in a bartizan on the NW corner. The castle was captured by Ludlow in 1651 and only restored to the O'Briens in 1666. William III confiscated the 57,000 acre estate of Donal's grandson the 3rd Lord Clare, and in 1691 Carrigaholt went to the Earl of Albemarle. He sold it almost immediately to the Burtons, who held the castle until the 20th century.

CARROWENA or CASTLE BAWN   R676832

This building on a tiny islet in Lough Derg was blown up in 1827 to prevent it being occupied by a group of illicit distillers who had previously resisted an attack against them with artillery. Prior to a recent restoration there remained only the northern half of the 8.5m wide building standing 8m high. The lowest level has an east-facing entrance and a fireplace in the NW corner. The second storey had an unusual groin-vault.

CASHLAUNNACORRAN   R579600

The name means Castle of the Weir, it being perched on a rock in the Shannon. Dating from perhaps c1600-20, it has gunloops under the windows. The entrance on the south side is placed 3.5m above the river to allow for high tides. During the siege of Limerick in 1690 the castle was abandoned by its garrison after being hit by cannonfire.

CASTLETOWN   R282979   C

The NW corner of a tower rises from a mound of debris. The second storey was vaulted, and the level below has two blocked north-facing loops and a loop in the angle between the main block and the west wall of a square projecting turret.

CLARECASTLE   R352743   D

The D-shaped tower 8.7m in diameter on the west side of the bawn formed part of a twin-towered gatehouse of a late 13th century castle of enceinte probably built by Thomas de Clare on the site of the earth and timber fortress of Robert de Muscegros. A square turret adjoins the tower and there is a fine late medieval ogival-headed loop at second storey level beyond the gateway. Also of that period, when the castle was held by the O'Briens and was eventually used by them as a dower-house, is a tower or bastion on the east side of the bawn. The castle was captured in 1558 by the Earl of Sussex and handed over to Conor O'Brien, 3rd Earl of Thomond. In 1643 the Confederate Catholics besieged the castle from February until it was surrendered in September. It also suffered a two month siege by Cromwell in 1651. He had it rebuilt and it remained garrisoned until 1677. Most of the bawn wall dates from the period 1703-1891 when the castle formed a barracks, and there is a Georgian house (now derelict) on the north side.

CLENAGH   R366650   C

This tower measuring 14m by 10m may be late 16th century since the vaulted basement contains a blocked kitchen fireplace and there were large upper windows of two and three lights and gables with attic windows set directly above the outer walls. However the third and fourth storeys look as if they represent a second building campaign set upon an older base. The entrance in the south end wall is covered by a gunloop from a guardroom in the SE corner and there is a sheela-na-gig nearby. The unusually wide spiral stair, now broken, lies in the SW corner. The second storey has a fireplace at the north end and the third storey has a fireplace on the west side. The bawn to the south has old walls on the east and west sides. The castle is first mentioned in the early 17th century as being held by the MacMahon family. They held it until the mid 18th century, when it was ruinous.

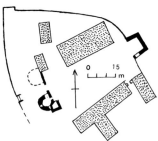

Plan of Clarecastle

Clarecastle

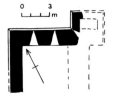

Castletown: plan

1st STOREY

Clooney: plan

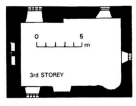

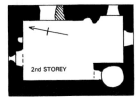

Castletown Castle

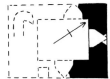

Cloondooan: plan

Plans of Clenagh Castle

Clenagh Castle

CLOONDOOAN   R380981   G

In 1586 Mahon O'Brien was killed by a musket ball whilst standing upon the battlements of his tower here defending it against a siege by Sir Richard Bingham, Governor of Connaught, which had already lasted three weeks. The other defenders then surrendered but were all killed and part of the tower was destroyed. Sir Henry Sidney had previously captured both Cloondooan and Ballyvaghan in 1569. The 8.5m long west end wall still stands 18m high with evidence of a vaulted basement and four upper storeys. The third storey was also vaulted, with a room in its east haunch. Nothing is currently visible of a semi-circular flanker on the east side of a bawn to the south.

CLOONEY   R421785

The east wall of this tower measuring 12m by 8.5m has mostly fallen. Built before the rest of the tower, it contained a spiral staircase and a tier of chambers over the entrance passage. The third level main room of the tower was vaulted. The north wall contains a fireplace at ground level and the chute of an upper storey latrine. Donough, son of Donard O'Grady is said to have built the tower in the mid 16th century. It was captured by Teige O'Brien in 1598 and passed to the Bindon family in the 1640s.

CLOONSELHERNY   M391003

Of this tower measuring about 12.2m by 7.4m there remain only the inner parts of the east end wall containing rooms over the entrance and a spiral stair in the SE corner, plus enough of the adjoining sidewalls to retain part of the vault over the lofty basement and the chute of the upper storey latrines on the north side. Part still stands 7m high. In 1580 this castle was held by Dermot O'Brien.

COLMANSTOWN   R119492

Most of the east end of this tower 7.8m wide by about 9m long set beside the Shannon estuary is now missing and there is no trace of the staircase. The second storey is a vaulted loft. In 1574 the castle was held by Tadhg MacMahon. In 1588 the MacMahons are said to have invited the crew of a Spanish galleon into the castle for a banquet that ended with the Spaniards' murder. The castle was mortgaged to the Burkes in 1627.

COOLISTEAGUE   R637639   C

The southern end of this five storey tower lying beside a modern house was built first and contains five levels of mural chambers over an entrance passage and guard room, plus a spiral stair with an angle-loop in the SW corner. The third and fifth storey mural rooms have ogival-headed loops facing south.

CRAGGAUNOWEN   R465736   E

A rock beside a small lake bears a polygonal platform about 25m by 20m with a mostly rebuilt low wall with a NE corner bastion flanking the entrance. In the middle stands a tower built c1550 by John MacSheeda MacNamara. It was later held by the O'Hartigans and Mulchonrys and was confiscated and slighted in the 1650s. Measuring 12m by 8.4m, the tower was restored in the 19th century, when the second storey was given bay windows facing west and south, the third storey was rebuilt, and a new attic room and parapet provided probably at a rather lower level than the originals. There was a further restoration in the 1960s when the castle was made into a museum and an exhibition crannog (recently burnt) was later created in the adjacent lake. The north end wall contains chambers over the rebuilt entrance and a spiral stair in the NE corner. The lowest level has a fireplace in the east wall and a wide arch to an adjacent block on the west. An arch supports a passageway from the stair to a latrine at an intermediate level.

Coolisteague Castle

Craggaunowen Castle

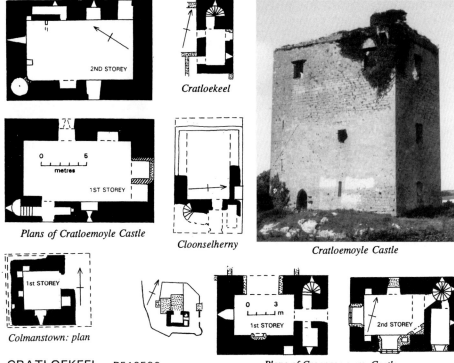

2ND STOREY

Cratloekeel

0   5
metres

1ST STOREY

Plans of Cratloemoyle Castle

Cloonselherny

Cratloemoyle Castle

1st STOREY

Colmanstown: plan

0   3
m

1st STOREY

2nd STOREY

Plans of Craggaunowen Castle

CRATLOEKEEL   R512590

A ruined house adjoins a thick end wall 7.8m long containing a spiral stair linking four rooms under a vault. The intended main part of the tower was never built. By 1615 the property was split between the original MacNamara owners and James Roche, but it later passed to the Dutch Protestant James Martin and was sold c1655 to John Cooper. It later passed to the Punch family, who occupied it until the early 20th century.

CRATLOEMORE or CASTLE DONNELL   R504588

Beside the Shannon to the SW of Cratloekeel is a bawn 30m by 24m with a low battered wall forming an arc on the south side, where there are traces of a ditch. A ruined later farmhouse lies on the west and on the north is a gateway, or perhaps the entrance doorway of a tower house.

CRATLOEMOYLE   R513593   D

This 16th century tower 17m high measuring 16.5m by 11m over walls 2.2m thick has vaults over the second and third of four storeys. An internal arch provides a thickening of the north end wall to contain mural chambers higher up, these being reached by a spiral stair in the NW corner. The lowest level was a kitchen with a fireplace in the east wall. It and another fireplace higher up use the same stack. Further north this wall contains a second storey latrine. There are circular bartizans on the NE and SW corners. Despite it being granted to Edward White in 1585, the MacNamaras held this tower until the last of this branch died in 1780, when the castle was sold to the Quins. In 1707 John O'Brien kidnapped the heiress Margaret MacNamara and forced her to marry him.

CREGMOHER or DRUMFINGLAS   R283866   D

An eminence is crowned by remains of the SW corner (still complete c1900) of a tower and the south wall and the 4m diameter SW corner flanker of a small surrounding bawn. It was held by Donnchadh Beag O'Brien who was hanged by the English for his part in the Desmond rebellion from the friary tower at Quin in 1584 after his bones had been broken.

DANGAN   R280643   D

The second and third storeys of this four storey ivy-clad tower on a rock have fireplaces on the west side and mural rooms in the east wall, the uppermost of which may only have been reached from above. The tower measures 11.2m by 9.5m and is entered through a wall 2.2m thick containing a straight stair leading to a spiral stair in the NW corner. A fireplace was later inserted into the embrasure of the west loop of the cellar. The tower was held in 1574 by Teige MacMahon and in 1600 formed a refuge for Lady Honoria O'Brien from the Desmond FitzGeralds. In 1641 it was granted to Sir Henry Ingoldsby.

DANGANBRACK   R426749

This MacNamara tower 14m long by 9.2m wide was probably originally built c1500 but if so it was remodelled c1600 since the lowest level has a kitchen fireplace at the far end and at the summit are four gables flush with the outer walls. There was no wall-walk as such but reached off the attic room in the roof above five full storeys were open defensive positions in the form of bartizans with pyramidal corbelling on two diagonally opposite corners and circular bartizans with double-stepped corbels on the other two corners. There is the usual tier of chambers and a spiral stair in an end wall.

Cregmoher Castle

Cregmoher: plan

Dangan Castle

Dangan: plan

Danganbrack: plan

Plans of Dangan Iviggin Castle

Danganbrack Castle

Derryowen Castle

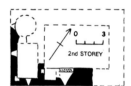

Derryowen: plan

DANGAN IVIGGIN   R455757

Hidden away in woodland is a fragmentary bawn about 36m square with gunloops in a 6.8m diameter flanker at the NW corner and a hall block 20m long by 11m wide on the south side, west of which the bawn projects further south. Projecting from the middle of the west side is a rectangular block 16.5m long by 12.2m wide over walls mostly 2.3m thick. The missing SE corner contained the lower part of a mural stair in the 2.6m thick east wall. Said to be the work of Cumheadha MacNamara (although attributed by Lewis in 1837 to Philip de Clare), this appears to be a 14th century hall house, later than others in North Munster, and significantly its crosswall and vaults appear to be original rather than later insertions, although there are two later dividing walls in the western part. Above the vaults there was just one large room, now fragmentary and very overgrown. Charles II granted it to Pierce Creagh but the castle was probably a ruin by then.

DERRYOWEN   R394954

Parts of the SE and SW walls still stand six storeys high, with evidence of a tier of chambers over an entrance passage blocked by rubble at the SW end and a spiral staircase in the west corner. The building was 8.4m wide and the SE wall was nearly 12m long until the east corner, with corbels at the top for a former bartizan, collapsed in 1990. The third level of the five storey main part has a fine fireplace and the fourth storey has remains of a passage being carried across the tower to connect a latrine with the staircase. In 1589 this O'Shaughnessy castle was acquired by George Cusack. In 1599 he was killed by the O'Briens of Leamaneh in revenge for George's execution (when sheriff of Clare in 1582), of Donogh O'Brien. In 1641 the castle was held by John Cookson.

DONOGROGUE   R054532   D

The lowest two storeys of a 16th century tower of the MacMahons of Clonderalaw forms the western part of an 18th century house built by the Hickmans. They held the estate from the 1650s until the 1790s, being succeeded by the Hodges family, whose arms appear over the original entrance in the east end wall. The house succeeded a lower late 17th century house of just one storey with attics in the roof, as depicted on Thomas Dineley's sketch of 1680, where the tower, which measures 13m by 7.5m, is shown at least five storeys high. The spiral stair in the NE corner was replaced by a straight flight of stairs in the 1840s and few other ancient features now remain.

DOONAGORE   R070957   C

In the 1970s this circular tower house 8.9m in diameter high above Doolin was restored and given new double-stepped battlements around a conical roof, and the fragmentary bawn 20m wide by 39m long (still nearly complete in 1878) was also then patched up. The bawn north side has remains of an outbuilding with a fireplace and latrine. The tower has four storeys with a pointed vault over the second. The staircases follow the curvature of the outer walls. Latrines are collected together on the east, which lies outside the bawn. The castle was held by Sir Daniel O'Brien of Dough in 1580 and was granted in 1582 to Terellagh O'Brien of Ennistymon. It was in MacClancy hands in 1590 and was forfeited after the 1641 rebellion, going to John Sarsfield. It later passed to the Gores, by whom it was repaired c1800, although it had become ruinous by 1837.

DOONBEG   Q962666   C

Only a 15m high fragment of the NE corner of a tower with a 2.2m thick north wall with a latrine-chute and traces of two vaults still remains. The castle remained intact and occupied by tenant labourers until just before much of it collapsed into the river in 1939. Originally a MacMahon seat, and about 8.8m wide by 13m long, the castle was later held by the O'Briens. In 1599 Daniel O'Brien was captured and imprisoned here by Tadhg Caoch MacMahon. Although Daniel was set free after a week his brother took a terrible revenge, bringing up artillery from Limerick to Doonbeg to force it to be surrendered, after which the garrison were hanged in pairs. The castle was granted to James Comyn in 1619, and was held by Loughlan MacCahane in 1642, but was back in O'Brien hands by the 1690s. It was occupied in the 1750s by Edmond O'Hogan, Sheriff of Clare.

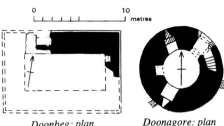

0   10
|_|_|_|_|_|_|_____| metres

Doonbeg: plan

Doonagore: plan

Doonmacfelim Castle

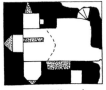

Doonmacfelim: plan

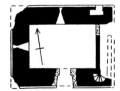

Doonmore: plan

Doonbeg Castle

Doonagore Castle

DOONMACFELIM   R071959

This ruined O'Brien tower with very high quality stonework beside Doolin village now only partly stands two storeys high. It measures 10.6m by 8.8m and has only a small basement because of the thick walls, although there are large embrasures containing loops. The storey above was divided into two rooms.

DOONMORE   Q971655   C

This tower measuring 11m by 8.3m stands on a low rock by the shore. The vaulted lowest storey with three loops is badly defaced, and at the east end the straight staircase from the entrance to the foot of the spiral stair in the SE corner has been destroyed, along with its outer wall. Off the spiral stair is reached a chamber in the southern haunch of the vault over the second storey. A passage in the east wall connects the stair with a latrine in the north wall. The upper parts of the SW corner, which was surmounted by a turret, collapsed c1905 and a few years later the walls above the upper vault were pulled down. Originally a MacMahon castle, it was owned in 1574 by Sir Donel O'Brien. It was in MacGorman hands in 1588, and in 1599 was captured by the Earl of Thomond in consequence of the activities of Tadhg Caoch MacMahon (see Doonbeg).

Dough Castle

Doonmore Castle

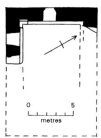

Dough: plan

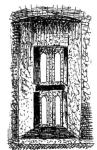

Drumline Castle   *Window shutters*   *Dromore Castle*
                                 at Dysert O'Dea

DOUGH   R094892   D

At the north end of Lahinch golf course, by the Inagh River, stands a 20m high fragment of the NW end wall and part of the SW wall of a tower once 13.5m long by 10m wide. The lack of vaults and the use of wooden lintels in the tier of windows suggest a date of c1600-40, but more massive walling in the very low basement could go back to the period around 1422, when Rory O'Connor of Dough was killed by his kinsman Felim. By 1548 the castle was in O'Brien hands, Sir Turlough being confirmed in possession in 1585, and his son Daniel O'Brien being Sheriff of Clare in 1643. Since he was a Protestant and had always supported the English cause his castle was spared the general slighting 1654-5.

DROMOLAND   R390706   H

The O'Briens of Leamaneh transferred to Dromoland in the late 17th century and eventually the bawn gateway from Leamaneh was re-erected here. The main building, now a hotel, but the seat of Lord Inchiquin until 1962, was entirely rebuilt in the 1820s. It contains a mahogany table thought to have come from a wrecked Armada ship.

DROMORE   R353865   A

The NE wall contains two levels of rooms over an entrance passage and guard room and a spiral stair in the north corner. At the summit there is a high chimneystack and corbels for a bartizan on the east corner. The chimneystack and lack of vaults in the main block suggest a date around 1600 for this round-cornered building 9.6m wide and once probably up to 14m long. This is confirmed by the inscription over the entrance recording its erection by the third earl of Thomond's second son Teige O'Brien and his wife Slaney.

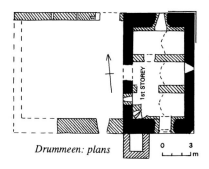

Drummeen: plans

Drummeen Castle

DRUMMEEN or BALLYCARROLL   R354850

This building measuring 12.8m by 7.8m appears to have been a thinly walled 13th or 14th century hall-house. The upper storey had its own separate upper entrance and four narrow windows, whilst there is a shouldered-lintelled doorway in the SW corner leading to a straight stair in the south wall up to the wall-walk. This doorway also gives access to a latrine in a turret added slightly later, its plank-centred upper vault indicating an early date. In a later medieval remodelling the old lower entrance was blocked up and a new entrance was inserted in the south wall. Both end walls were thickened and two crosswall inserted to carry a series of three vaults over the lowest level, whilst a spiral stair linking the levels was inserted in the SW corner. A small bawn with a north-facing gateway (now a ragged hole with a drawbar slot) was created by building walls between the hall-house and the shore of a lake (almost dried up) to the west. The greater thickness of the south wall of the bawn suggest an intention to add a domestic wing on that side.

DRUMLINE   R429647   D

This building measures 14.2m by 9m and rises about 16m to a wall-walk now lacking its parapet, but gables with windows for an attic in the roof stand still higher. Three corbels remain of a machicolation over the broken entrance in the north end wall. The staircase in the NW corner is broken and so are the vaults of the lofty lowest two levels. From the stair a passage carried on an arch leads past a chamber of the entrance to a latrine in the east wall. The top storey has remains of two-light windows on all four sides.

DYSERT O'DEA   R283850   E

The tower built c1470-90 by Diarmaid O'Dea was captured in 1570 by the Earl of Ormond, passed to the Neylons in the early 17th century, and has now been restored to serve as an archaeology centre. It measures 12.3m by 8.6m over walls 2.1m thick and has one end wall still thicker to contain the entrance, staircase and a tier of chambers. A loop off the passage to the stair pierces the doorway jamb. The fourth storey has windows of two lights cusped both above and below a transom.

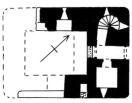

Dromore: plan

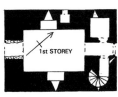

Dysert O'Dea: plan

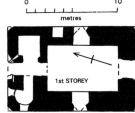

Drumline: plan

Fahee Castle

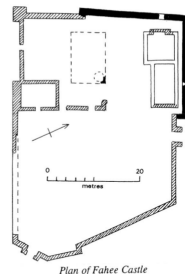

Plan of Fahee Castle

Faunarooska

Garruragh: plan

ENAGH or STACKPOLE'S COURT   R497707   D

Only a low fragment remains of the eastern half of the north wall of a tower about 12m long by 7.2m wide, and not much remains of a range later extended to the north of its NE corner. From this range another two storey wing extended westwards, leaving just a 1.3m gap between its south wall and the north wall of the tower. The west end of this range survives, with a projecting breast containing upper and lower fireplaces.

ENNIS   R338772   C

The Old Ground Hotel incorporates a much-altered tower belonging to the O'Brien earls of Thomond and measuring 9.6m by 7.5m. The town's east gateway may have adjoined it and the town jail certainly lay alongside it. By the 19th century there was a whole complex of buildings here. The second storey contains a fireplace transferred here in the 1960s from Dromoland, but originally from Leamaneh. There is mention of the leasing of a second castellated building in Ennis which had formed part of the former abbey.

ENNISTYMON   R128886   H

A much-altered tower house said to have been built c1560 by Domhnall O'Brien forms the NE corner of the Falls Hotel, most of which was built by Edward O'Brien in 1764, although there is further ancient work at the south end, where an outbuilding has been incorporated. The tower retains a vault and one loop, now blocked internally.

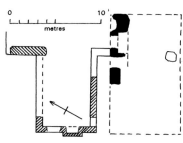

Plan of Enagh Castle

Garruragh Castle

FAHEE   M302996

Surrounding the debris and a low fragment of the NE corner staircase of a tower is a 1m thick and 2m high bawn wall, probably the work of two periods and perhaps fairly new in 1617, when Owney O'Loughlin died in possession of Fahee. The bawn eastern extension with north and SE gateways may date from the mid 1650s, when Fahee went to Blakes. Part of a parapet with gunloops remains on the west and there is a square SW corner turret. The northern part of what may be the oldest part of the bawn is filled with a house, the west gable of which, with a fireplace, still stands 7m high.

FAUNAROOSKA   M144053   C

At the southern corner of a bawn about 25m by 20m with a ruinous drystone wall lies a tower about 7.3m in diameter, now mostly collapsed on the west but still two storeys high on the east with evidence of an upper vault and one crossloop facing east set in walling 1.4m thick. Until the late 20th century part of it still stood four storeys high. The castle guarded a track known as the Green Road high up on the west side of the Burren and was held by Fernandus MacFelim in 1641. It was later given to James Aylmer and Henry Ivers.

GARRURAGH   R510505   C

This MacNamara tower measuring 11.2m by 7.7m with gables above the third storey appears to be comparatively late since the only vault in it is that over the guard room beside the entrance in the south wall, above which is the usual tier of chambers linked by the spiral stair in the SW corner. A joint above the battered base shows that most of this end was built first. The castle was given to Philip Bigoe in 1641. The inserted wall in the lowest main room may date from the 1840s, when the castle served as a fever hospital. A roof probably of that period inserted over the second storey has mostly collapsed.

Faunarooska Castle

Glensleade Castle

Falls Hotel, Ennistymon

GLEN   R138876

The 10.5m long north wall with a central latrine chute still stands 10m high of a tower once about 8m wide with a tier of lesser chambers over an entrance in the east wall. Much of the building collapsed c1890. It was built by the O'Connors, although in later years they occupied it only as tenants of the O'Briens.

GLENCOLUMBKILLE   M324000

Of a bawn wall at Glencolumbkille North the only remaining parts are those which formed three walls of a hall block at the SE end with corbels of a bartizan on the south corner. The tower in the middle of the NW side is represented only by part of the NW wall with a latrine chute and a pile of rubble. The NE end contained the entrance, staircase and mural chambers. There seems to have been a second castle nearby at Glencolumbkille South (316997) and there is confusion as to whom owned what but both seem to have been O'Loughlan seats handed over to the Blakes after the 1641 rebellion.

GLENINAGH   M193104   B

The O'Loughlins occupied this late 16th century tower until 1840, hence its good state of preservation. It measures 8.5m by 6.7m over walls 1.1m thick and has a spiral staircase in a south facing SE corner wing with at its foot the entrance doorway protected by a box-machicolation high above. The other three corners have circular bartizans. Above a subterranean pit-prison are four full storeys and there was an attic in the roof, which has gables flush with the outer walls. Evidence of slightly later alterations or a change in design during construction are the fireplaces created out of former window embrasures in the west end wall of the second storey and in the south wall of the fourth storey.

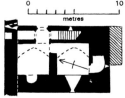

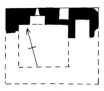

Plans of Gleninagh Castle   *Gragan: plan*   *Glen: plan*

Gragan Castle

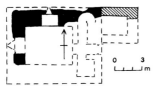

Glensleade: plan

Gleninagh Castle

GLENSLEADE   M230010

Only footings remain of the north and west walls of a bawn 24m by 16m containing a tower about 10.2m long by 8m wide of which the north wall remains, with traces of a spiral stair in the NE corner. Beyond this corner are slight remains of a projecting wing which may or may not have enclosed the east-facing entrance. The castle was confiscated from Turlough O'Loughlin in 1595 and granted to Edmond Barret, although the O'Loughlins were back in residence by 1601, if indeed they ever left. They were forfeited after the 1641 and replaced by the MacNamaras.

GRAGAN   M204036   E

The 1.5m thick and 4m high north and west walls of a bawn 33m by 23m still retain a parapet with gunloops. Added against the north wall, and utilising a latrine chute within it, is a tower 11.4m by 7m containing two rooms at ground level, the southern room having a double-splayed loop and mural chamber in the south wall. The east wall contains the entrance and a flight of steps up to the a spiral stair in the SE corner, which was later reinforced by a buttress on the south side. Above a pair of vaulted lofts forming the second storey was a fine room with a fireplace on the west side, a latrine in the NE corner and a three light window with double transoms in the south end wall. In a recently completed restoration the missing parts of the bawn were reinstated and the ruined uppermost parts of the tower house replaced with wooden-framed structures. The castle was held by Malaghlin O'Loughlin at his death in 1623. It was confiscated after the 1641 rebellion and granted to George Martyn of Galway, although the O'Loughlins remained in occupation. One of them married George's daughter Alice and their son used the surname Martyn. In the meantime the Martyns left Galway and built a house near Gragan Castle.

INCHICRONAN   R397866

Only the northern half of the east wall, with a latrine-chute adjoining the lost tier of chambers at the south end, now remains of a 15th century O'Brien castle on the neck of a promontory. In 1585 it was held by Henry O'Grady. In 1641 a party of dispossessed O'Gradys besieged the Roughans, then holding tower as tenants of the Earl of Thomond, who came to their relief, although the castle was captured as soon as he left. Conor O'Brien was defeated and mortally wounded in a battle against Ludlow here in 1651. A Cromwellian garrison held it in 1652-6. See page 16.

INCHIQUIN   R270901

On a shelf of rock above the lough is a wall up to 4m high around bawn 39m long by 26m wide, the west side being filled by a 17th century house with its upper storey mostly in the roof. The house has several ground-level fireplaces with projecting chimneystacks on the east side. Lower walls remain on the northern side of the bawn, where there was a gateway. A fragment of the north wall of a tower house about 7m wide, with remains of a stairwell in the NE corner, lies in the NW corner of the bawn. This tower is thought to have been built by Teige O'Brien shortly before he became King of Thomond in 1461. His descendant Murrough submitted to Henry VIII of England and was created Earl of Thomond in 1543. In 1559 Donogh O'Brien, the heir under Gaelic law, was besieged here by Conor O'Brien, the heir under English law, but the garrison was relieved by the Earl of Desmond, who defeated the forces of the earls of Clanricard and Thomond. Donogh's brother changed sides and served as sheriff of Clare in 1570, his nephew Murrough being in possession of the castle at Inichiquin in 1574. During the O'Donnell campaign of 1599 the castle was attacked by the Maguires. in the 1640s Murrough O'Brien, Lord Inchiquin served as President of Munster. He was known as Murrough of the burnings because of his ferocious attacks upon Catholics, and was later created Earl of Inchiquin.

Kilkeedy Castle

Inchovea Castle

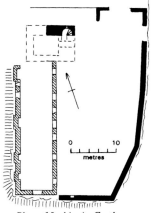

Plan of Inchiquin Castle

Inchiquin Castle

INCHOVEA or TOORMORE   R221905

Dramatically set upon a shale outcrop with a stream to the south and east is the east half of a tower 7.8m wide with remains of two vaults, the uppermost having chambers in the haunches reached by steps from the third storey east corners. The fifth storey with a mullioned window seems to be an addition, heightening the tower to over 20m. A similar window below is inserted into the embrasure of an older window. In 1580 the castle was held by Tadhg, son of Murrough O'Brien, but by 1654 it had passed to William Neylon.

KILKEEDY   R371952

The 10.4m long north wall stands three storeys high with broken corbels for a continuous machicolated parapet. The top storey has a fireplace and a latrine reached from the former stair in the SE corner by a passage carried on pyramidal corbels. The east wall contains three levels of rooms over the entrance passage, the second level being at the height of the main vault. From this room a doorway was later broken through to give access to a loft created under the vault. In 1584 Kilkeedy was held by Mahon O'Brien, son of Lord Inchiquin.

KILKISHEN   R486722

The east end wall containing a spiral stair with an angle loop in the NE corner and a tier of chambers over the entrance was built first and remains almost complete with a vault over the fifth level and a machicolation over the entrance. The northern half of the remainder of the building stands to the same hight, with a two-light window at fifth storey level, but only fallen fragments and rubble remain of the southern half after a collapse in 1989. The tower measured 12.4m by 7.2m and the fourth storey main room was vaulted. Said to have been built c1500 by Sean MacNamara, the castle was forfeited in the 1650s and granted to Henry Ivers. It was later sold to John Cusack. See front cover picture.

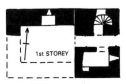

Kilkishen: plan

Plans of Kilkeedy Castle

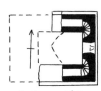

Inchovea: plan

KILNABOY   R270914

Beside the River Fergus is a wall 1.2m thick enclosing a bawn 31m long by 24m wide known as de Clare's house although there is no certain connection with the family of that name. There is a gateway with a drawbar-slot on the north, a postern on the south towards the river, a small turret containing tiny rooms projecting south at the SE corner and there are also tiny rooms in an internal thickening of the wall at the NE corner. The west side was filled by modest house. Only cut stones reset in outbuildings remain of an earlier tower held in 1574 by Sir Domhnall O'Brien located to the NE at 272918.

KNAPPOGUE   R441718   E

Medieval banquets are held in this five storey tower which has 19th century battlements and surrounding ranges of one and two storeys also of that date. The four-light window on the top storey is 17th century and most of the other windows more recent. There is a vault over the third storey. Built in 1467 by Sean MacCon MacNamara, the castle was briefly held by the Smith family in the mid 17th century, but otherwise remained a MacNamara seat until sold to the Scotts of Cahircon in 1800. It was sold to Lord Dunboyne in 1855 and fell into ruin after being sold to the Land Agency in 1927. The building was restored after being purchased by the Andrews family from Texas.

LEAMANEH   R235936   C

The castle is first mentioned in 1550 when it was granted to Donough O'Brien, who was hanged by the English in 1582. It has a thick end wall of c1500-30 with a wide spiral staircase, an entrance passage with rebates and drawbar holes for inner and outer doors, and a tier of chambers equipped with gunloops, angle-loops at third storey level, and a window with twin cusped lights at the sixth storey. The intended main body was never built and a century elapsed before a stronghouse of four storeys and an attic was grafted on to the older part to create a building 24m long by 10.5m wide. The house has its own entrance and tiers of four-light mullion-and-transom windows. There were offices and a kitchen on the ground floor and living rooms above. At the far end from the older part is a bartizan on one corner and a wing on the opposite side, the only part to have a wall-walk. In front was a bawn with a gateway which was removed to Dromoland in the 19th century. It was dated 1643 with an inscription recording its erection for Conor O'Brien and his wife Maire Ni Mahon, about whom legends abound. After Conor was mortally wounded in the battle of Inicronan in 1651 she saved her lands for her son by marrying a Cromwellian officer. She is said to have kicked him out of an upper window after he was rude about her first husband. Beyond the road are remains of a large walled garden.

Leamaneh Castle

Knappogue Castle

Interior of Leamaneh Castle

Liscannor Castle

LISCANNOR   R063880   D

Recent collapse has destroyed most of the east end, which was built first and contained chambers over the entrance passage, and of the main block only fragments remain two storeys high with traces of a vault at that level and a latrine-chute on the south side. Miraculously the NE corner staircase still remains complete right up to the wall-walk over the fifth storey, with a second storey angle-loop. The castle was built by the O'Connors but was later taken over by the O'Briens, being held by Sir Donald O'Brien of West Corcomroe in 1574. From 1712 the earl of Thomond leased it to the Fitzgeralds but it was ruined by 1837. The tower is 9.2m wide and was once about 13m long.

LISMEEHAN or MARYFORT   R525807

The defaced base remains of Rory MacNamara's tower of c1420-40 measuring 11.5m by 7.5m. It had an east entrance, a SE corner staircase and latrines on the north side. The castle was held by Connor O'Brien, 3rd Earl of Thomond in 1563, but was back in MacNamara hands by the 1570s. It was superseded by new house nearby c1710.

Liscannor: plan

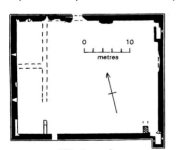

Kilnaboy: plan

Plan of Leamaneh Castle

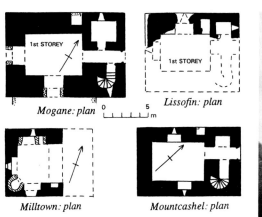

Mogane: plan   Lissofin: plan

Milltown: plan   Mountcashel: plan

Mogane Castle

LISSOFIN   R480784   D

The 2.2m thick and 10.2m long NW wall of a tower once about 8m wide still stands four storeys high with a two-light window on the top level, from which was reached a latrine in the haunch of the vault below. The entrance and mural chambers lay in the NE wall so the spiral staircase must have been in the east corner. A MacNamara possession, the tower was held in 1570 by Ellen, widow of the Earl of Thomond and was ruinous in 1611, although it was recorded as in repair in 1703.

LISSYLISHEEN   R206990

Walls up to 1.8m thick and 1m high with little or no mortar surround what appears to have been a western outer bawn 14m wide and 31m long added alongside an inner bawn about 28m by 19m now only represented by buried footings. What little remains standing of the tower in the SW corner is buried in a 4m high pile of debris. The castle was held by the O'Loughlins in 1574 but was occupied by the O'Davorens in 1585. They were still here in 1659 despite forfeiture in favour of the King family, but in the 1680s the castle was held by Thomas Wallcott.

MAGOWNA   R283819

The remaining three storey high fragment of the north wall is mostly covered in ivy and difficult to see or reach because of surrounding vegetation. Said to have been built c1480 by Donn Chadha, son of Tadhg O'Dea, the tenure of the castle was divided in 1612, when Daniel O'Brien had the use of the cellar and the room above, whilst Donnchadh Grana had the use of the three uppermost levels. There was a similar arrangement in 1642.

MILLTOWN or BALLYMULLEN   R464806

Three ivy-covered walls still stand five storeys high of a tower measuring 9.5m by 7.2m with diagonally set chimney-stacks rising above the outer faces on the west and north sides. These are additions, the fireplaces in the vaulted basement and the level above being insertions into the embrasures of north-facing loops. A latrine-chute adjoins them. The east wall containing the staircase and a tier of chambers over the entrance was built before the rest. It collapsed in February 1981 and is now only represented by a mound of rubble. Turlough O'Brien, Sheriff of Clare, held Ballymullen in 1570. He was hanged in Galway in 1581, his son Tadhg was hanged in 1596 for plundering Ormond. In the 1650s the castle was confiscated from the O'Briens and given to Philip Bigoe.

Lissylishen Castle

Mountcashel

MOGANE R404708 D

Now back in use as a residence, this tower measuring 13.2m by 9m built c1490 by Donal Conner remained occupied by gamekeepers until the late 19th century. It has a vaulted basement, a lofty pointed vaulted room above with an east fireplace and a top storey with an east fireplace and two-light windows. The east end wall containing the entrance has an extra level corresponding to the lower vault and behind the extra room is a passage leading from the SE corner spiral staircase to a latrine in the north wall.

MOUNTCASHEL or BALLYMULCASSELL R475689 C

This tower on a rock above the road is said to have been built by Conor na Srone O'Brien, who died in 1470. It measures 11.2m by 7.2m and contains five storeys with a vault over the fourth storey, which has a latrine in the NW wall. The NE wall contains a tier of chambers over the entrance and a spiral stair lies in the east corner rising 2m above the wall-walk some 16m above ground. The top storey has windows of two lights facing NW and SW. Recent repairs include replacing of lower quoins of the south and west corners.

Milltown or Ballymullen Castle

Lissofin Castle

MOY   R096843   C

Lying within a bawn about 29m by 20m with its interior filled in to a depth of about 1m to make a platform 3m high is the two storey high west wall of a tower 14m long, the southern end of which appears to be older than the rest. North of the bawn, perhaps only originally reached from within it, is an underground well. This was the seat of the barony of Ibrickan (Hy Brecain) created for the Earl of Thomond's son Donough O'Brien in 1543, although the MacGormans had held lands here in the 1390s. During the rebellion of 1641 the castle was held by Captain George Norton as a tenant of Daniel O'Brien of Dough. In 1719 the castle was granted by the 8th Earl of Thomond to Augustine FitzGerald.

MOYREE   R379902

The presence of bee-hive shaped flankers fairly close to the NW and SE corners of the tower house set in the SW corner of a shovel-shaped bawn 48m by 33m, suggests that there was once an inner bawn enclosing the tower north and east sides, the other sides being set above low cliffs. Little remains of the SE flanker and not much of the bawn wall. The main part of the tower has a vaulted basement and two upper storeys below a second vault, but within the same height the north end wall contains four rooms over the entrance passage. At the top there is just one large thinly walled room with two-light windows on all sides, an arcade upon pyramidal corbels at the south end, and the spiral stair projecting into the NE corner. Below this level the stairwell and a small vaulted room have angle-loops. An arch over the north end of the second storey main room supports two levels of low passages leading across the building to latrines within the same height as the main third storey room. The western loop of the cellar was later made into a fireplace. A lightning strike upon the tower in 1899 damaged the second storey fireplace, wrecked the upper part of the staircase and killed several pigs in the cellar and two horses in the bawn. The castle was held by the Earl of Thomond in 1584.

MUCKINISH   or   CASTLETOWN SPANCILHILL   R389796

Two lofty storeys under a vault remain of a tower measuring 12.6m by 9.4m with latrines in a turret at the north end of the NW wall. The SE wall contains a straight stair rising from a broken doorway at the south end. The castle is said to have been built by Rory, son of John MacNamara in the 15th century. It was held in 1570 by Brian O'Brien but in 1602, after either he or a relative of the same name was hanged by the Earl of Thomond, the castle passed to John King, although it later reverted back to the MacNamaras.

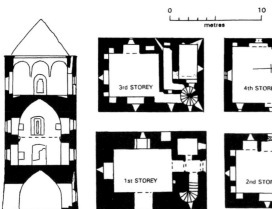

Plans & section of Moyree Castle

Mountcashel Castle

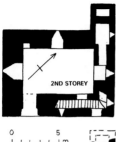

2ND STOREY

1ST STOREY

Plan of Moy Castle

Muckinish: plans   *Muckinishnoe*

Muckinishnoe Castle

MUCKINISHNOE M277092 C

Half of an O'Loughlin tower house 8.6m wide and probably once about 11m long stands on a rock by Poulnaclogh Bay. It contained five storeys with vaults over the second and fourth storeys, with a mural chamber in the haunch of the upper vault. The third storey had a latrine in the west wall. There are traces of a small thinly walled bawn on either side. In 1603 the castle was held by Daniel Neylon, Bishop of Kildare.

Tower base at Quin

Moy Castle

Moyree Castle

Fireplace in Newtown Castle

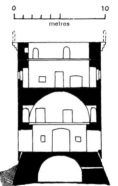

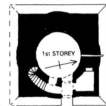

O'Brien's Castle

Newtown: plans & section

NEWTOWN   M217066   E

This recently restored 15m high 16th century tower with dome vaults over the first and third of five storeys has a cylindrical superstructure 9m in diameter rising above a massive square pyramidal base. One corner contains a guard-room beside the entrance passage. At the join of the two shapes are triangular recesses in the apex of which are gunloops in the sills of second storey windows commanding the whole of the base, a very ingenious design. Other gunloops include those with double bottom roundels commanding the angles of the pyramidal base. At the summit are four restored machicolations, one of them commanding the entrance. The fourth storey room has a fireplace and mullioned windows with hoodmoulds, one of them being of three lights. The walling containing the spiral staircase bulges out into this thinly-walled room. A gallery has replaced the fifth storey.

O'BRIEN'S   R409832   D

This building measuring 13.5m by 8.4m is said to have been built by Turlough, Bishop of Killaloe c1460-80. The topmost level was built in one campaign but lower down the four storey main block with vaults over the second and fourth storeys was built after the north end wall. This part has five levels within the same height and a spiral stair in the NE corner which is complete except for a short section near the base. At the level of both main vaults arches carry passages from the staircase to latrines in the west wall. This wall also contains the fireplaces, probably all later insertions. The tower remained thatched until the early 20th century, hence its comparatively complete condition.

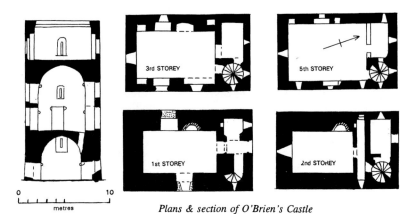

Plans & section of O'Brien's Castle

QUIN   R419745   A

In 1280 Thomas de Clare built at Quin a court 33m square enclosed by a wall 3m thick with circular corner towers up to 12m in diameter. The interior must have contained timber framed ranges of buildings around a small open court. In 1286 the garrison killed an Irish chief named O'Liddy and in revenge Cuvea MacNamara captured and destroyed the castle in 1288. By 1350 a church had been built within the ruins, although it was mostly rebuilt in the 1430s when Sioda Cam MacNamara founded a Franciscan friary here. The gateway and one corner tower have vanished, and only an outline remains of another tower, but the lower parts of the NE and SE towers and the east wall between them still remain to the east of the friary buildings. The thick south wall of the friary church probably also contains original work, through which many 15th century openings have been pierced.

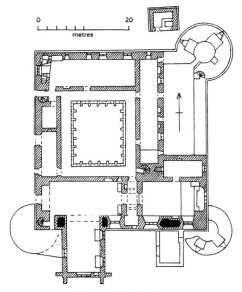

Plan of Quin Castle

Newtown Castle

RATH   R268859   D

The 10m long east wall still stands three storeys high with evidence of vaults over the lower two levels, fine two-light windows set in round-arched embrasures on the top storey, and a latrine chute against a join showing the east end was built first. Just one step remains of the spiral stair in the SW corner. The tower and the bawn extending to the north and south lie on a rock in a marsh beside a lough. In 1574 the castle was held by Muircheartach Garbh O'Brien. It passed to Bishop Rider in 1617.

RATHLAHEEN   R433667

This 16m high tower measuring 13.7m by 8.9m has two storeys under a vault and another two above it, the entrance and mural chambers being in the east wall. The broken spiral stair in the NE corner has an angle loop at second storey level, where it has access, via passage carried on an arch over the lowest room, to a latrine in the south wall.

RINEROE   R633624

Little remains of the east wall containing chambers over the entrance. The western part added later to make a structure 7m wide and about 9m long stands four storeys high with a vault over the third storey. This room was reduced to being a small loft since its east end was divided off as a passage making a latrine in the north wall accessible from the spiral stair in the SE corner.

ROSSLARA   R533816   C

This was once a fine tower 14.4m long and at least 10m wide, but only the west wall remains in a rather defaced condition lower down. The south end seems to have contained unusually wide subsidiary rooms, and probably also the entrance and staircase, but there were also mural rooms in the northern corners at a level corresponding to the vault over a lofty basement. The second storey also seems to have been vaulted.

Rossroe Castle

Rathlaheen Castle

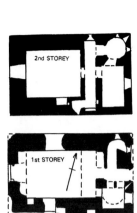

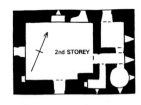

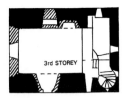

Plans of Rathlaheen Castle

0   10
metres

Plans of Rossmanagher Castle

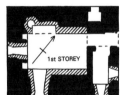

Plans of Rossroe Castle

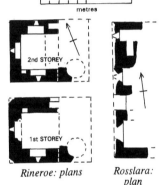

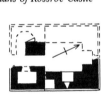

Rineroe: plans   *Rosslara: plan*

Rosslara Castle

Rath: plan

ROSSROE   R450697

Sioda MacNamara is said to have built this tower now lying in a farmyard before 1402, making it one of the earliest in Clare. It measures 12.3m by 9.6m and has three storeys with two levels vaulted. There are separate entrances to the lowest two storeys, and the broken spiral stair only began at the second level. A service stair (now blocked and obscured at the bottom) was inserted into the SW end wall c1600-40 when a new range was added beyond it. At the same time the SE wall was given a wide new window embrasure and the lowest room made into a kitchen with a fine fireplace with a joggled lintel set within an inner skin of walling inserted to carry a new lower vault, in which there is a hatch. The second storey is lofty enough for there to be a mural chamber above its entrance within the same height, whilst a low chamber is tucked under the base of the spiral stair. In 1564 Conor O'Brien, 3rd Earl of Thomond escaped from the castle when it was attacked by a group of his kinsmen, although a hundred of his men were killed.

ROSSMANAGHER   R466629

This tower measuring 13.8m by 9.4m has a vaulted basement with an inserted fireplace and two upper storeys. A passage to the second storey main room from the stair in the SE corner leads past doorways to a latrine on the south and to the third of five levels of subsidiary rooms in the NE corner. An added range has left only its roof-mark.

SHALLEE   R289794

There are two-light windows in the fifth storey room which lies over a low vaulted loft, alongside which are passages in the sidewalls. The loft has a SW angleloop, and there are corbels for a former bartizan on the SE corner. The entrance and staircase must have been in the north end wall, which has been destroyed, perhaps the result of Cromwellian slighting. On the east side is part of the thin wall of a surrounding bawn with a ditch 9m wide and 2.5m deep. In 1574 the castle was held by Brian Dubb O'Brien, who had been pardoned in 1568-9.

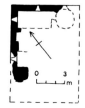

Skaghard: plan

SHANMUCKINISH   M263104   C

The north wall of this 16th century O'Laughlin tower which passed to the Blakes in 1622 collapsed c1900. The tower was 7.8m wide and probably 10m long above an unusual splayed plinth. The inside is closed off by a crosswall of later date. There were four storeys with vaults over the second storey and the lofty third storey, there being chambers in the haunches of the upper vault. At the top there is a machicolation in the centre of the remaining end wall whilst the sides had a continuous machicolated parapet. The end wall contains a three-light window with a transom and hoodmould.

SKAGHARD or CARROWNAGOUL   R349981   D

Parts of the north and west walls still stand five storeys high with traces of the staircase in the east corner. The tower was about 7.8m wide and probably nearly 11m long. In the NE wall a tier of chambers lay over the entrance passage, which is now blocked by rubble. Mahon MacBrien O'Brien sublet part of the castle to Connor MacDonough O'Brien of Leamaneh in 1598, reserving the attic room for himself.

Rossmanagher Castle

Shallee Castle

Skaghard Castle   *Shanmuckinish Castle*

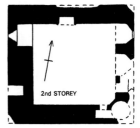

Shanmuckinish: plan   *Shallee: plan*   *Smithstown: plan*   *Teerovannan: plan*

SMITHSTOWN   R147931

A recently restored 16th century tower measuring 12.5m by 8.2m lying by a stream has four storeys with vaults over the second and fourth. The third storey has a fine fireplace and NW and NE angle-loops, off one of which are gunloops. On the second storey an L-planned latrine chamber is tucked in behind the lowest of a series of rooms over the entrance in a thick end wall. The castle was held by Richard Wingfield in 1612. It was owned by Conor O'Brien of Leamaneh in 1649, when it was captured by Ludlow for Cromwell. It passed to the MacNamaras c1703 and was occupied until c1850, although by then the fifth storey was ruinous.

TEEROVANNAN   R542759   D

Although lofty and impressive, this 15th century tower measuring 14.2m by 13m over walls up to 2.8m thick at ground level is much defaced and the vaults over the lofty first and second storeys have gone, whilst little remains of a spiral stair turning anti-clockwise in the SE corner. The second storey has a fine fireplace in the north wall, remains of two loops with large embrasures facing east and another embrasure on the west, where there is a also a doorway to a mural chamber set more than 2m above the main floor level. The third storey may have been subdivided. It had a latrine in the SW corner, a recess in the NW corner, a window facing west and two windows in each of the north and east walls. In the 1580s the castle was held by Donal Reogh MacNamara. See p 54.

TIRMACBRAN   R262889

The 8m wide southern part with a fine east-facing doorway with a hoodmould (towards a former bawn upon a cliff) still stands five storeys high. The lack of vaults and the square-headed two-light window with a hoodmould near the top suggests late date, so the building held by Mathun O'Brien in 1574 may have consisted of just the older north end, which has been totally destroyed, perhaps through slighting in the 1650s.

TROMRA   R007733   G

One of the ships of the Armada of 1588 was wrecked close to this well preserved 15th century tower which was then one of several seats of Sir Turlough O'Brien. He executed the sixty survivors that came ashore. A castle is mentioned here in 1215, when it was handed over to the Archbishop of Cashel, but the O'Briens were in possession by the 1270s. Edmund O'Flaherty was eventually executed in Galway for the killing of the then owner Peter Ward and his wife and son during an attack on the tower in 1642. The tower was returned to the Earl of Thomond in 1652 and was later occupied by the Burton family. It measures 12.2m by 8.8m and still has all four walls complete to the wall-walk some 16m up. The destruction of the vaults over the lofty lower two storeys may have saved the tower from collapse, since the base is much defaced and the straight stair in the south wall from the entrance to the broken spiral staircase in the SE corner has lost its outer wall. The SE corner has corbels for a bartizan and the NE corner contains two levels of latrines and rises up as a turret more than 4m higher than the rest. The second storey has remains of an inserted fireplace in the west end wall, which contains no windows.

Tirmacbran Castle

Teerovannan Castle

Tromra Castle

Tuamgraney Castle

Tyredagh Castle

Tromra: plan & section

Urlan Beg: plan

Tirmacbran: plan

Tuamgraney: plan

TUAMGRANEY   R636830   C

Above the south-facing doorway of this tower measuring 10.2m by 8.4m there is a recess rising up to where there is a machicolation from the wall-head. The SW corner contains the staircase and the north wall contains a mural chamber at the level of the second storey, which is vaulted. The third storey has a fireplace surmounted by a chimneystack.

TYREDAGH   R463824   D

This tower measuring about 12m by 8.4m. was described as ruinous in 1613. Very little remains of the east wall containing chambers over the entrance and a spiral stair in the SE corner. The north and south walls survive high enough to support the basement vault, whilst the west wall is still four storeys high, with a segmental arch to widen it to carry a wall-walk. There is a latrine-chute on the north side.

URLANMORE   R382663   &   URLANBEG   R385664

Only a 3m high long length of the east wall has survived the collapse of most of the castle of Urlanmore in 1999. Until then it was 18m long, 7.8m wide and had wall paintings of animals in a chamber in the 17m high southern end. A fallen fragment of it retains evidence of arcading. In 1580 it was held by Murtagh MacClancy. Just 200m to the north lies the vaulted basement of a second building, Urlanbeg, measuring 9.6m by 6.4m, now lacking its SE end wall. The general appearance of the SW wall, which contains a doorway with a drawbar slot, suggests that the building once extended further on this side.

OTHER CASTLES IN COUNTY CLARE

AHERINAGH R614657 Low fragment on hilltop. Inaccessible because of vegetation.
BALLYGANNER R220947 Debris pile and NE corner two storeys high. Traces of vault.
BALLYMASLEN or CASTLETOWN R386777 Rubble mound of MacNamara castle held in
    1570 by William Neylon. Part of window head reset in nearby wall.
BEAL BORU FORT R696743 Tree-covered ringwork or unfinished motte is a relic of an
    Anglo-Norman raid into Thomond. Overlies 11th or 12th century ringwork.
BUNAKIPPAUN R404976 Fallen fragments only of tower held by Lord Inchiquin in 1580.
BUNAVORY R478503 Rubble mound. Seat of Clancys, hereditary judges (brehons) of
    Thomond. Held in 1574 by Donough MacClancy. Held 1641 by Sir Roland Delahoyde.
CAHER R690826 Fragment of 1.7m thick south wall of MacNamara tower and 2m high
    fragments of wall of tiny bawn to west and south. Totally obscured by vegetation.
CAHERCORCAUN R273869 Footings, debris and fallen fragments of O'Brien tower. Parts
    reset in farm outbuildings and stone dated 1627 upon derelict farmhouse.
CAHERHURLEY R608815 2m high fragment of MacNamara tower on rock outcrop.
    Passed to Burkes in 1622. Tenanted by Matthew Hicks in 1641.
CLONMONEY R427616 Motte rising 8m to summit 9m across and triangular bailey 55m
    by 23m to north. Site of tower held in 1580 by Earl of Thomond.
COOLREAGH R595830 Rubble mound covers cellar of MacNamara tower. Granted to
    Conor O'Brien 1560. East wall 9m high in 1839. Latrine chute visible in 1980.
CORBALLY R430781 Road cuts across 2m high mound 20 across. Footings were visible
    in 19th century. Went to Pierce Butler after Conor MacNamara was forfeited in 1641.
DOONOGAN R086735 Buried base and rubble pile of O'Brien tower on 20m high rock.
    Granted to 4th Earl of Thomond in 1585, and to James FitzNicholas Bourke in 1618.
DRUMMAAN R768888 Defaced, overgrown base of tower 8.6m by 8.1m. Bawn traces.
DRUMMIN R575625 West wall 3m high at roadside now part of shed in garden of house.
DUNLICKY Q835576 Footings of MacMahon promontory castle. 15m high tower 5m by
    4m fell in 1879. Had wing walls on either side with gateway south of tower.
FEENISH R344624 Ruined tower orientated north-south on island in Fergus estuary.
FINLOUGH R437705 Very slight overgrown remains beside track up to house.
FOMERLA R450791 Two low fragments, one fallen, behind a modern house.
GRANAGHAN R426693 Fragmentary lower parts of tower 7.5m wide behind house.
    East wall contains spiral stair, entrance passage and small guardroom.
INCHMORE R301754 3m high fragment of stairwell on west bank of river near bridge.
    Held in 1574 by Conor McClancy.
KNOCKALOUGH R139634 Vegetation obscures remains of tower on crannog. Seat of
    "liar and deceiver" Turlough MacMahon "who by one stroke killed his wife and child".
LECARROW R028004 Slight remains of MacNamara castle above cliff on north side.
LOUGH INCHIQUIN R272896 Marked on old maps as a small tower house on island, but
    supposedly built in 1281 by Turlough O'Brien. Excavated in 19th century.
MOANOGEENAGH R571761, MOUNTSHANNON R146509 & NEWTOWN R622625:
    All three of these towers are now reduced to footings buried by piles of rubble.
PORTLECKA R339859 Footings of tower about 7m by 11m now lacking north end.
POULADOONEEN or BALLYHERAGH R018878 Slight traces of possible tower on stack.
RATHFOLAN R400692 Now a pile of debris, but two storeys survived fifty years ago.
SCATTERY ISLAND Q972512 Fragment of Keane castle begun c1570 at south end of
    island. Vaults still in use for storing turf in early 20th century.
SMITHSTOWN R148941 High fragment of west wall of MacNamara tower lying in
    industrial estate. Traces of staircase well and third storey vault.
TULLAGH R197914 Wall of O'Brien tower within bawn 30m by 24m stood complete
    until 1930s. 2m high inner SE corner remains with traces of latrine-chute.
TURKENAGH R344920 Slight remains of tower house. No recorded history.
The remains in a housing estate at Knockanaura R349784 are mostly or entirely 19th
    century. There are coastal batteries at Lakyle 094506 and Doonaha West 886529.
Carrigoran R392677 is a ruinous late 17th century FitzGerald house.

CASTLE SITES IN CLARE

BALLYKETT R009570 Keane castle NE of Kilrush. Granted to Sir Daniel O'Brien in 1604. Leased by Lord Clare to Henry Hickman in 1668. Gone by 1816.

BALLYMURPHY R202981 Remains of O'Loughlan tower removed c1980. Held by Prendergasts in 1601 but later passed to the O'Briens.

BEALNALICKA R312854 Site of O'Dea tower probably demolished in 1790s. Stone eye of doorway set in front garden wall of modern house.

BOHNEILL R208856 Traces of bawn, last remnant of tower gone since 1900, but loops jambs and sills remain in shed. O'Brien castle later held by the MacBrody family.

CAHERMACREA R345880 Reduced to rubble mound in woodland. Ruin remained in 1839. Hugh Oge O'Hehir was pardoned by Elizabeth I's government in 1591.

CAHERMURPHY R106663 Fragment of MacGorman tower & earthworks now gone.

CAHERRUSH R020769 Site of coastal tower of O'Brien earls of Thomond. Surviving corner fell c1900, leaving only pile of debris and a modern dry-stone pier.

CARROWDUFF R242869 Debris of O'Brien castle. Stones from it at house to north.

CASTLEBANK R581614 19th century house on site of castle of Earl of Thomond besieged in 1642.

CASTLE DERMOT R042146 Site of castle on crannog.

CLOGHANSAVAUN R755151 Site of MacMahon promontory castle which fell either in 1755 or 1802-3. Passed in early 17th century to Sir Daniel O'Brien.

CLONDERALAW R140558 Remains of MacMahon tower on rock removed c1945-70.

CLONROAD R346779 16th century O'Brien tower demolished by 1730 on site of castle of 1284. Captured and garrisoned by Earl of Ormond in 1570.

CLOONMORE or CARROWMEER R390741 Site of tower held by Shane Riogh MacNamara in 1570.

CRAGBRIEN R302694 Reset corbels from MacGyleragh tower in outbuildings.

DRUMULLAN R458703 Site of MacNamara tower on rock by lough.

FINNER R045726 No remains, but ruin survived until at least 1893.

FREAGH R033816 Fragments of loops of former O'Brien tower by shore in fieldwall and nearby boathouse. Part stood until 1910. Granted to Morrish Hickie in 1656.

GORTBOYHEEN or CASTLE MAEL M275054 Last slight remains demolished in 1970s.

ISLANDMAGRATH R350709 Cut stones from Magrath tower in later buildings.

KILKEE R303852 Arch on site of tower of the MacBrodys, poets and historians.

KILKEE R879460 Site of tower held by MacSweeneys as tenants of the MacMahons.

KILNAMONA R274801 Catholic church of c1840 on or near castle site.

KNOCKANALBAN R045726 Ruined MacBrody tower on crannog survived until after 1893. Held by Dermot MacGorman in 1642.

MOYARTA Unlocated MacMahon castle probably near Carrigaholt. Vanished by 1839.

MOYHILL R239852 Stones from O'Hagan castle in nearby buildings. One is from fine archway of c1600 of bawn. Westropp mentions datestone of 1637 in nearby house.

MOYHULLIN R255847 Cut stone in fieldwalls only relics of O'Dea castle.

TULLA R493798 Remains by graveyard had gone by 1911. Held in 1574 by Dunell Reogh MacNamara. Recorded as ruinous in 1611, 1613 and in the 1730s.

TULLAMORE R116921 Silage pit on site of tower held in 1574 by Sir Donal O'Brien of Dough. Briefly held by Neylon family in 1580s. Rubble pile was removed c1980.

TURLOUGH R284050 Loose cut stones on wide debris mound. Conveyed by Owney O'Loughlan to John Lynch of Galway in 1590. Later passed to Neylons.

OTHER CASTLE SITES: Ballyconneely R374694 & R282696, Ballynabinnia R274801, Ballygirreen R374687, Ballykelly R546725, Ballyvaghan M230082, Carrowduff R242869, Castle Dermot R042146, Clashmore R584864, Cragbrien R302694, Deerpark R464742, Edenvale R317740, Inismacowney R288594, Knockanimana R353743, Knockanoora R349784, Knocknagarhoon R815551, Lecarrow R583864, Maghera R240877, Mountallan R531743, Querrin R925541, Slievenacarrowduff R244866, Toonagh R441776, Trough R587645

POSSIBLE SITES: Cloonmore R390740, Coolreaghmore R606823, Moynoe R668848.

CASTLES OF COUNTY LIMERICK

ADARE   R470468   E

Recently cleared of vegetation and consolidated by the Irish Board of Works, this fine castle beside the River, Maigue at Adare belonged to the Kildare branch of the FitzGeralds. It was forfeited after the rebellion of 1534 and granted in 1541 to the Earl of Desmond, but was later returned to the earls of Kildare. The castle is first mentioned in 1226 as a possession of Geoffrey de Marisco. The wall 1.6m thick around the north side of the D-shaped inner ward 26m across upon a probably older ringwork and the D-shaped open-backed tower facing west are thought to date from c1200. Also of that period is the smaller and older of the two halls on the south side of the outer ward, facing the river. This hall is 16.5m long by 9m wide and has windows with two round-headed lights. It lies above a basement, later subdivided, and has a wing containing latrines projecting at the SW corner into the river. Only slightly later is the tower keep measuring 13m by 10.8m on the east side of the inner ward. It has corner turrets which project from the side walls only. It was originally of three storeys with the basement only reached from above by a trapdoor, but in the 15th century the lowest level was provided with its own entrance and vaults carried upon an inserted crosswall, whilst the storey above was given a new doorway in the north wall. The upper parts of the southern half are missing, possibly the result of slighting, although there is no evidence of any other damage being done to the castle during that period. The square gatehouse on the south side of the inner ward is probably late 13th century. The castle was in a poor condition in 1329 and the realigning of the SW wall of the inner ward may have been part of the repairs carried out c1340.

Just north of the hall of c1200 is an internally projecting west gatehouse, the outer part of which is early 13th century, whilst the inner part may be later 13th century. East of the hall are footings of a kitchen, beyond which is a ruinous aisled hall measuring 22m by 10.5m probably of the late 13th or early 14th century. Towards the river it has windows between buttresses, whilst the other side has a porch. On the east a passage leads between a pair of service rooms to a kitchen, now very ruined but retaining one oven. A later medieval wall up to 1.7m thick and 3.5m high to the well-preserved wall-walk surrounds an outer ward containing the halls and extending 45m eastwards of the keep. It has gateways facing east and north and part of a ditch or flanking towers or turrets.

East side of outer ward at Adare

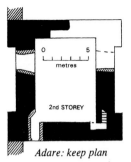

Adare: keep plan

0   5
metres

2nd STOREY

Keep & inner ward at Adare

Keep, Adare

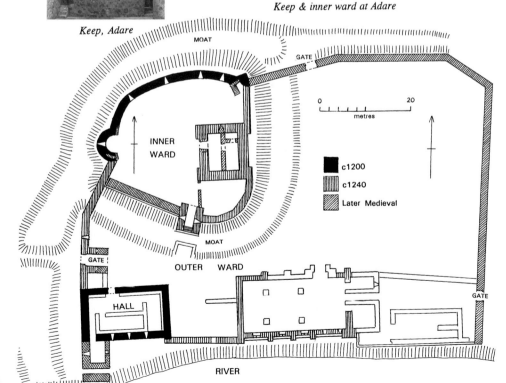

Plan of Adare Castle

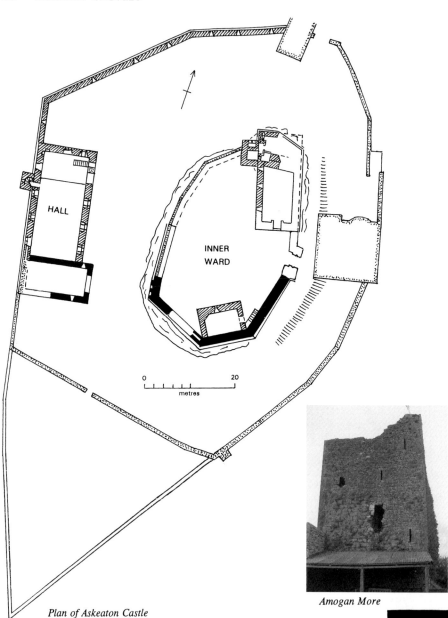

HALL

INNER
WARD

0 _____ 20
metres

Plan of Askeaton Castle

Amogan More

AMOGAN MORE   R396414   C

There are two storeys under a vault in this tower measuring 8.4m by 6.6m, and two upper levels reached by a stair from the north facing entrance. Probably built by the Sarsfields, it was granted in 1588 to the Billingsleys.

Amogan More

ASKEATON R341502 E

This castle on a rock in the middle of the River Deel is thought to have been founded c1200 by William de Burgh, although the earliest surviving parts probably date from later in the 13th century. It passed to Thomas de Clare in the 1280s and in 1318 was granted by Edward II to Robert de Welle. By 1348 it had passed to the Earl of Desmond. In the 15th century it was remodelled and served as one of the main seats of the earldom until in April 1580 it was surrendered to the English commander Pelham after a two day bombardment, after which it was handed over to the Berkeleys. In 1599 the Earl of Essex relieved the castle after it had withstood a 247 day siege by the forces of the "Sugan" Earl of Desmond. The castle was surrendered to the Confederate Catholics under Purcell in 1642 and was captured and slighted by Cromwellian forces in 1652.

The river skirts the walls of a lozenge-shaped outer ward 60m wide and 120m long. They are mostly 15th century work and are reduced to footings south of where a thin modern wall crosses the site, while at the north end there is a gap where there was once a gatehouse. A 13th century block on the west side contained a ground floor hall about 15m long by 9m wide with a service passage at the north end leading out between a buttery and pantry to a lost detached kitchen, whilst at the south end is a fragmentary cross-wing containing a chamber over an office. The block was remodelled in the 15th century to provide a new upper floor hall with two-light windows with seats in embrasures overlooking the river and a new north end wall slightly extended the building. The stair turret on the west side may also be of that period, whilst the solid floor of the hall lies upon vaults inserted later which are supported on a crosswall and a row of two piers.

Only fragments remain of a polygonal wall probably of 13th century origin around an inner ward 40m long by 24m wide. It has a gateway on the east and latrine chutes just west of a square building at the south end. The north end contained a three storey building containing a lofty hall over a basement and a low third storey, the upper rooms having mullioned windows and fireplaces in the west wall. Only the lofty and impressive western end remains of a four storey chamber block at the north end with vaults over the second and third storeys and latrines in a projecting wing facing west.

Nothing remains of a second castle at Askeaton mentioned in 1580 under the name Short Castle and later held by the Nashes.

Hall block in outer ward at Askeaton

Askeaton Castle

3rd STOREY

3RD STOREY

1st STOREY

1st STOREY

Ballyallinan: plans

Ballingarry: plans

0   10
metres

Ballinveala Castle

Plans of Ballinveala Castle

BALLINGARRY   R414361   C

This lofty de Lacy tower measures 11.4m by 8m at the level of the hall on the third storey where a large window embrasure has a piscina on one side and has evidently contained an altar. Other embrasures have seats and two-light windows. A spiral stair in a corner leads down to the entrance and cellar. The stair to the battlements is squinched out over the re-entrant angle between the end wall and a wing containing a latrine and bedchamber. The tower was repaired in 1821, served as a barracks during local disturbances of 1827, and was later used as a hospital.

BALLINVEALA   R530460   D

The east end wall contains a spiral stair with a keyhole-shaped NE corner loop and three chambers over the entrance passage, the topmost level being vaulted, and the second level having a SE corner loop. Although the O'Briens seem to have never completed the 8m wide main tower the surviving part remained in use until the late 19th century.

BALLYALLINAN   R346377   D

There are vaults over the second and fourth levels of this tower measuring 13m by 9.3m and the fifth storey has rooms in bartizans on the east and west corners. Reacheed from the altered entrance facing NW, a spiral stair in the north corner still rises as far up at the third storey, which has remains of three windows and a fireplace on the NW side. The NE wall contains a tier of vaulted rooms over a deep recess at ground level. Named after the original O'Hallinan owners, the castle was surrendered to the English in 1569. It was later held by the MacSheehy family, originally mercenaries serving the Desmonds.

BALLYBRICKEN   R653459

Of a tower measuring 11.2m by 8.7m there remain two very ruinous lower storeys under a vault. Not much remains of the east wall which contained a spiral stair in the SE corner and mural chambers of the entrance passage. An old sketch shows a three storey house beside a four storey tower.

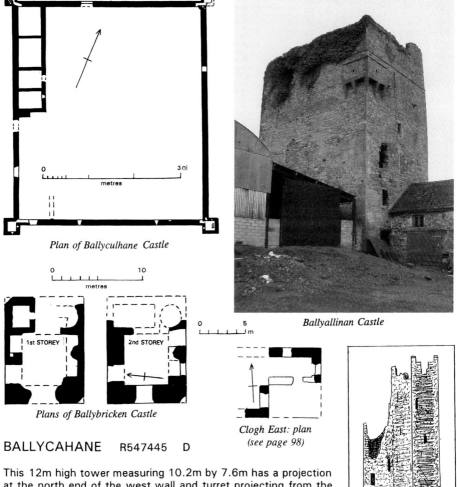

Plan of Ballyculhane Castle

Plans of Ballybricken Castle

Clogh East: plan
(see page 98)

Ballyallinan Castle

Ballingarry Castle

BALLYCAHANE R547445 D

This 12m high tower measuring 10.2m by 7.6m has a projection at the north end of the west wall and turret projecting from the west end of the south wall. The first and third of four storeys are vaulted and there are remains of a large east window at second storey level, but the interior is now inaccessible. A gable and wallwalk survive on the north end wall. The castle was a Berkell seat from 13th century until sold in 1655 to George Peacock.

BALLYCULHANE R462540 D

An ivy-mantled wall about 3m thick and 6m high surrounds a bawn 45m long by 40m wide. There are square corner towers containing tiny vaulted rooms and spiral staircases. On the south and SW are windows and fireplaces of former two storey ranges of apartments. Buildings on the NW side are comparatively modern. There is said to have once been a 9m wide wet moat fed from the River Maigue. The castle belonged to the Purcells until the 1650s. After it was stormed by the English in 1581 some 150 women and children were put to death.

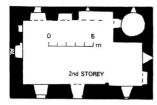

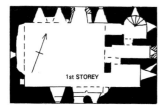

Plans of Ballynahinch Castle

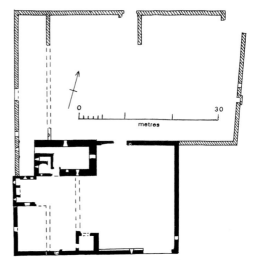

Plan of Ballygrennan Castle

BALLYEGNYBEG   R281421

This tower measuring 10.8m by 8.8m was forfeited by the Walls for their part in the 1583 rebellion. It was held by William Stephenson in 1587, but had passed to the Stephensons by 1598. Two storeys remain under a vault, the lower level having two double-splayed loops. A straight stair rises up from the north-facing entrance doorway, now blocked up.

BALLYGLEAGHAN or CURRACHASE   R407512

Ivy and vegetation obscure most of the features of a much-ruined tower on the front lawn of an 18th century house but gunloops are visible in the lowest level. Either this building or another now vanished further south was burnt in 1580 by the Earl of Desmond to prevent English forces under Carew from occupying it.

Ballygrennan Castle

BALLYGRENNAN R635350 D

The earls of Kildare are said to have had a castle here but the existing tower may date from after 1583, when Ballygrennan was granted to William ffox. It measures 13.6m by 8m and has two levels below a vault and two lofty upper storeys with large two and three-light windows with hoodmoulds and transoms. Most of the parapet surrounding a fifth storey attic still remains, with square bartizans on the NE and SW corners. The only part to have a battered base is the part of the west end wall adjoining the wide spiral staircase (now destroyed) in the SW corner. The entrance, now destroyed, faced south beside the staircase. Of a house of c1600-20 added on this side there remain only the south end wall with a wing extending east of it and most of a wing projecting west adjoining the SW corner of the older tower. Walls were soon added to enclose a small back court with its own doorway west of the house and a SW corner bartizan, and a bawn 20m square was laid out to the east of the house. The ffox family seem to have lost Ballygrennan in 1621, although they had recovered it by 1657. By then a large outer bawn 38m long by 26m wide had been added on the north side. It has a gateway facing north and corbels for a SE corner bartizan. Doorways were broken through from the lower levels of the tower to give access to an outbuilding filling the west end of this outer bawn, perhaps an addition by the Evans family, to whom the castle was sold in the 1660s. Fireplaces on the upper level suggest it was a stableblock with accommodation for grooms and servants above.

BALLYNAHINCH R707280 C

Margaret Grant, widow of Gibbon FitzGibbon, erected this castle in the 1620s or 30s. It measures 16m long by 10.2m wide and has at the east end an entrance passage set between a vaulted room and a wide spiral staircase (now broken) in the NE corner. The main rooms are not vaulted and there are remains of mullion-and-transom windows with hoodmoulds and also gables set on the outer walls. The only gunloop commands the entrance, later blocked up and replaced by another entrance (with its own murder-hole) on the north side. The second storey has a fine fireplace on the north and the third storey a fireplace on the south, whilst subsidiary rooms at the east end also had fireplaces.

Ballyegnybeg: plan

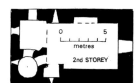

Ballygrennan: upper floor plan

Ballyegnybeg Castle

Interior of Ballynahinch Castle

Beagh Castle

Ballyvoghan Castle

BALLYVOGHAN   R276408

A wing 3.8m wide projecting 2.4m at the east end of the south wall of this tower measuring 11.1m by 11.3m contains at second storey a latrine reached off the much damaged straight flights of stairs rising in the south and east walls. Nothing now survives above the vault over the second storey, which has a mural room in the SW corner, originally with a murder-hole covering the entrance (now blocked) below it.

BALLYVORNEEN   R700470   D

This tower with walls 1.5m thick was held by the Lansies and then the Mauncells and remained occupied until the late 20th century. An old drawing show it accompanied by a later range. Derelict, much altered and obscured by ivy, it lacks features of interest.

BEAGH   R358570   G

There were vaults over the first and third levels of this tower measuring 10.4m by 8.2m but only the lower vault remains intact and the rooms over the entrance in the east wall are very ruinous, and the spiral stair in the SE corner has been damaged, although the top is still accessible. The fourth storey is arched over at each end. The second storey has remains of a fireplace on the south and a latrine in the NE corner. Three vaults of uncertain date extend westwards from the tower and a range of later outbuildings to the south may incorporate or replace a bawn wall cutting off the low coastal promontory site. A possession of the knights of Glin, Beagh was given to William Drury in 1578.

BOLANE   R443534   D

This castle on a commanding rock was held by the Shanes in 1583 but in 1591 was granted to the Carters. It was held by William FitzGerald from 1625 until 1655. The SW corner of a tower 9.2m by 7.8m still stands four storeys high. The lowest level is vaulted and has a gunloop opening off the embrasure of the southerly of two loops in the west wall. Not much remains of the east wall which contained small chambers over a flight of steps leading from the entrance to a spiral staircase in the NW corner. See Page 69.

Bolane Castle

Bourchiers Castle

4th STOREY

2nd STOREY

2nd STOREY

2nd STOREY

1st STOREY

1st STOREY

0   5
metres

Bourchiers' Castle, Co Limerick

Beagh: plans & section

Ballyvoghan: plans

0   30
metres

Black Castle, Lough Gur: plan

BOURCHIERS or CASTLE DOON   R647410   D

This seat of the Earls of Desmond was confiscated by the English Crown in the 1580s and granted to Sir George Bourchier, whose descendants, later earls of Bath, held it until 1641, hence the present name. It has five storeys, plus a chamber below ground, and measures 15.6m by 10.9m. The entrance lies in the south end wall containing a tier of chambers which was begun before the rest of the tower. Three and two light windows on the third and fourth storeys suggest a 16th century date. The castle covered the NE approach to Knockadoon, which was almost enclosed by Lough Gur. Hidden in shrubs at R628405 is Black Castle, which protected the southern approach to Knockadoon. It consists of a 2.4m thick length of curtain wall with a gateway in the middle. An island in the lough to the NW at R639407 is said to have remains of a third castle called Knockfennell.

Bruree Lower Castle

Brittas Castle

BRITTAS   R722506   D

Beside the Mulkear River are fragments of a 13th century castle of the Burkes. There is a circular corner tower 8m in diameter with a dome vault and a later latrine turret, the two being united higher up by a pair of squinch arches. In the tower are arrowloops with blank or dummy oillets at top and bottom and on either side. A curtain wall extends to the river and footings of a wall lie along the river bank with signs of a domestic range against it. A second circular NW corner tower survived until at least the 1840s. In 1607 Sir John Burke of Brittas was hanged at Limerick for having a priest say mass in his house here.

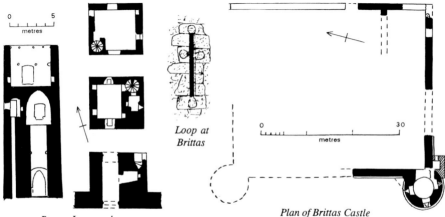

Loop at Brittas

Plan of Brittas Castle

Bruree Lower: plans

BRUREE LOWER   R543311   D

Originally held by the O'Donovans, Bruree was later held by the Lacys until 1641. A bawn said to have measured 45m across now only retains parts of its south and east walls. Centrally placed on the south side is a 16m high tower 6.3m by 5.8m which contained a gateway passage with a void space above, a vaulted room with seats in window embrasures and a latrine beside it at third storey level, and a fourth level on top, the upper levels being reached directly from the court by a spiral stair in the SW corner. There are said to have been two other towers, one of which collapsed during a gale c1830.

BRUREE UPPER or BALLYNOE   R550303   C

In the churchyard of a derelict Protestant church lies an ivy-clad four storey tower measuring 11m by 7.8m. The lowest level has double-splayed loops and an entrance (currently hidden) facing north, from which rises a narrow spiral stair in the NE corner. The third level has a vault. Above the second storey the SE corner is missing. This de Lacy castle was captured in 15698 by Captain John Warde.

BULGADEN EADY   R641302   D

In a field behind a school lies a tower measuring 11.4m by 10m with a entrance facing SE and two double-splayed loops in the lowest level, whilst the second storey is vaulted. Nothing remains of the upper storeys reached by a straight stair in the SW wall. The castle was held by Eady Lacy in 1583. It was confiscated c1652 and given to Captain Massey.

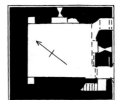

Bulgaden Eady: plan

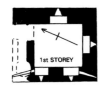

Bolane: plan

0   10
|_|_|_|_|_|_____|
       metres

Bruree Upper: plans

Bulgaden Eady Castle

CAHERELLY   R659439

The NW, SW and SE corners of this O'Heyne tower measuring 10.4m by 7.8m still stand 18m high, with a stair in the SE corner still serving all five levels. The second and fourth storeys once had vaults and the fifth storey still has a room within a square bartizan on the SW corner, whilst the east wall contained a tier of subsidiary chambers over the entrance. A gunloop in the bartizan has a square hole at the base and an oillet higher up. A second tower nearby had vanished by 1900.

CAPPAGH   R390451   D

The northern half of a 21m high tower measuring 12.1m by 8.7m built c1460-80 lay within an inner bawn 17m square of which the north and west walls survive, the corner between them being chamfered off. The west side lies upon a rock face and the other three sides were enclosed by an outer bawn up to 10m wide, although not much now remains of the south wall and there is gap on the NE beyond a small round turret. The central tower was vaulted on the second and fourth of five storeys and had a fireplace in the north wall of the third storey. One fine window, wider than usual, remains at fifth storey level, where the west end was arched over in the same manner as at Beagh, like Cappagh a seat of the Knight of Glin. There was a tier of mural chambers over the entrance in the east wall, and a spiral stair in the SE corner. The castle passed to Sir William Drury in 1578. It later went to Ullick Browne and then in 1587 to Gilbert Gerrard.

Caherelly Castle

Carrigareely Castle

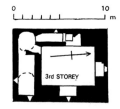

Carrigareely: plan

Cappagh Castle

CARRIGAREELY   R665504   D

This tower measuring 10.6m by 8.2m lies on a rock with a sheer drop of 6m on the west side and a drop of 1.5m on the south, so that a two storey range later added on that side had an upper storey almost at the same height as the lowest storey of the main tower. This end contains a tier of mural chambers over the entrance passage and there is a spiral staircase in the SW corner. Not much remains of the main tower above the vault over the third storey. The west wall contains a fireplace on the second storey and a latrine reached from the staircase on the third storey. The castle was owned by the Burkes but was usually occupied by the O'Dalys as tenants.

Caherelly: plan

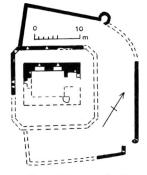

Plan of Cappagh Castle

Cappagh Castle

Carrigogunnell Castle

CARRIGOGUNNELL   R499552   G

This castle on a volcanic crag above the Shannon estuary was a major seat of the O'Briens although probably founded by the de Burghs and then held by the earls of Desmond. In 1536 it was surrendered to Lord Deputy Grey after being battered by cannon, and Edmund Cahill and his garrison were all hanged, but the castle was later recovered by the O'Briens. In 1650 it was taken over by Cromwellians under Captain Wilson, who built a stable in the bawn, but in 1655 the castle was sold to Michael Boyle, later Archbishop of Dublin. In 1691 a Jacobite garrison of 150 men surrendered the castle to William III's forces and shortly afterwards General Ginckel had it blown up. The heart-shaped outer enclosure extending down the slope and containing a barn on the east side is 15th century, although the triangular projection flanking the entrance with gunloops is a 16th century improvement. The northern wall of the oval inner court 30m by 20m on the highest part of the site is 13th century. Here lay a hall over two cellars. In the 15th century a four storey tower with the lower rooms hexagonal in shape was added east of the hall, and beyond is a block of two storeys containing a suite of private chambers with large windows and fireplaces. Between these two parts are remains of a spiral staircase.

CASTLE CONNELL   R660625   D

On a 6m high vertical-sided rock near the Shannon are overgrown fragments of a 13th century de Burgh castle with a court measuring 48m by 30m with at least one circular tower. This building or its predecessor was destroyed in 1261 by Conor O'Brien. John Burke, 2nd Baron of Castleconnell was murdered in London in 1592 by Captain Arnold Cosby, with whom he was to fight a duel. The castle was surrendered to a Cromwellian force in 1651, and William, 6th Lord Castleconnell subsequently lost most of his estates. In 1691 Captain Barnwell surrendered the castle to a Williamite force. It was blown up and the 8th Lord was attainted as a Jacobite, dying fighting in France in 1697. See p75.

13th Century

14th –15th Century

16th Century

0   40
metres

GATE

Plan of Carrigogunnell Castle

Carrigogunnell Castle

Castle Connell

Two views of Carrigogunnell Castle

Castle Hewson

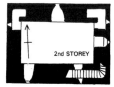

Castle Hewson: plans

CASTLE GARDE   R793495   D

In 1654 this former possession of the earls of Desmond was held by Henry, Earl of Bath. His widow leased it to the Baylee family in the 1660s. Shortly after the marriage of Grace Massy to one of the O'Gradys of Guillamore in 1823 the five storey tower was remodelled and a two storey wing added to it. Of about the same time is most or all of the court in front entered through a gateway flanked by a circular tower.

CASTLE HEWSON or BALLYENGLAND   R370499

Standing on a low crag (visible on the west side) is a tower measuring 11.7m by 9.2m with three storeys below a barrel-vault, above which are modern battlements reached from the south-facing entrance by straight flights of steps in the south and east walls. The second storey has three windows, a latrine in the NW corner and a small chamber in the NE corner. Recent investigations in the lowest room have revealed a stair in the north wall down to a lower level partly excavated in the rock. Although the tower lies empty without any floors and the adjacent house has now also been left empty, adjoining outbuildings to the north remain inhabited. Thomas England was pardoned by the Crown in 1581 and 1590 but his son was hanged and attainted and the castle later passed to the Hewsons.

CASTLE MATRIX   R351412

In 1487 James, 9th Earl of Desmond was murdered here by his servants on the instigation of his brother. Edmund Spenser and Walter Raleigh occupied the castle in 1580. It was granted to the Southwells, who added a wing in 1610. The Irish captured the castle in 1641, and the Cromwellians took it in 1651. There are vaults over the second and fourth of four storeys but there must originally have been a fifth storey above, in which case the existing open bartizans on the SW and NE corners must have once contained rooms opening off the top storey. The east wall contains six levels of small rooms, the extra two levels corresponding to the vaults over the main rooms and being reached of the SE corner spiral staircase. Almost all the windows were widened in the 19th century and other alterations seem to have included moving the entrance from the east wall to the north. The tower measures 13m by 8.7m, was again renovated in 1970 and remains occupied.

Castle Mahon

Castle Garde

CASTLE MAHON   R319311

This tower measuring 13.4m by 10.3m is obscured by ivy externally and very defaced and cluttered with derelict sheds internally. A stair in the NE corner linked three unvaulted levels each with fireplaces in the west wall. There were subsidiary rooms over the destroyed entrance facing east. The estate belonged to the bishops of Limerick but the castle most likely dates from the period after the Reformation.

Castle Connell: plan

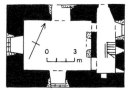

Plan of Castle Matrix

Plan of Castle Mahon

Castle Matrix

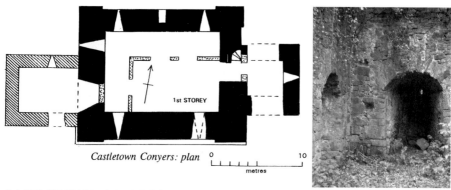

Castletown Conyers: plan

Castletown Conyers

CASTLETOWN CONYERS   R444300

A driveway up to a house bisects a wing 7.6m wide projecting 5.6m from the east end of a hall-house measuring 18m by 13.8m with broad pilaster buttresses projecting from each ends of the north and south walls, the latter being 2.9m thick above a battered base. Four basement loops remain fairly complete but a fifth is broken out. There is the lower part of a spiral stair beside passage leading to the wing, whilst the middle of the north side has the chute of a latrine from the destroyed upper storey. Until given to the Conyers family after confiscation in the 1650s this was the main seat of the MacEnery family.

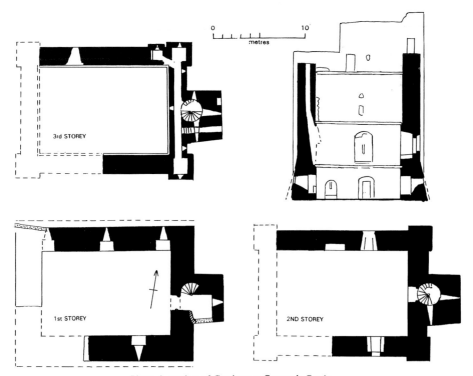

Plans & section of Castletown Coonagh Castle

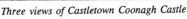
Three views of Castletown Coonagh Castle

CASTLETOWN COONAGH   R824479

Although later held by the O'Briens, this is a spectacular Norman keep of c1200 with its east end still standing over 20m high, although only footings remain of the west wall and the promontory site has no obvious remains of any outworks. The keep was 18.6m long by 13.4m wide over walls 2.1m thick above a base batter extending up as high as the wooden floor of the main hall. This room has a damaged fireplace on the north and a complete round-headed window with embrasure seats on the south. The level above has a window facing north but may not have been a habitable space in the original design. A latrine projecting from the north wall at that level is awkwardly reached off a gallery in the east wall which is itself reached by a spacious spiral stair in a turret projecting from the middle of the east wall. Off the gallery a passage extends out to where there must have been some sort of wooden balcony high up on the outer face of the building. At each end of the gallery are small square rooms within corner turrets rising from the battered base. The rooms, gallery, passage and staircase all have clear signs of their vaults being constructed with a centring made of planks, evidence that all these parts are a part of the original design and not later additions or alterations. In fact the only certain later medieval feature is western jamb of a blocked south-facing doorway in the central turret. Above the stair this turret contains two upper levels, and the wall-walk of the main building was reached off a second spiral stair in the SE corner.

Castle Troy

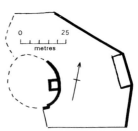

Plan of Croom Castle

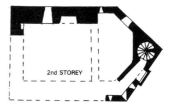

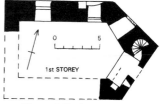

Plans of Castle Troy

CASTLETOWN WALLER   R387556

A house lies on the site of a castle of the Waller family. Furnishings damaged or plundered after the castle was captured by the Irish in 1642 included "eleven downe and feather beds, 6 flocke beds with boulsters, pillowes, blacketts, ruggs and caddoes....candlesticks, chamberpots, stills..... Hangings for a large dyning room and two chambers, of tapestrie, and divers other hangings" plus curtains, 2 turkish carpets, a clock and a chest of books.

CASTLE TROY   R627586   A

The 18m high east end of this 10.4m wide tower of the MacKeoughs of Glenkeen is built out as a prow containing the sprial staircase with a tier of sizeable vaulted rooms behind it, whilst other passages and small rooms lay over the SE facing entrance doorway. The result is a very rare five-sided building with a greatest length of 16.5m. The SE corner has an angle-loop at second storey level and corbels for a bartizan containing a chamber at fourth storey level. The main part of the tower further west contained rooms about 6m square, the lowest level being vaulted and the second level having a fireplace on the north, but this part is much ruined by the loss of the SW corner and most of the south wall. On the NW corner this part also had a room in a bartizan at fourth storey level.

CLONSHIRE   R423447   D

The vault in this tower measuring 9m by 7m blocks the original stair and may have been inserted when a wing containing a new entrance and spiral stair with a hole between the two was added in the 16th century. This part has a caphouse higher than the main block. Later on another, lower, three storey wing was added at the other end. The castle was held by Jason Crowe in 1641, and by Captain Piggott in 1655 in right of his wife.

Croom Castle

CROOM   R511409   C

Castle Troy

The castle has a fragmentary tower about 6m square lying within the eastern part of an polygonal inner bawn about 23m across, the western part of which has gone. Chambers against the southern part of the bawn have also gone but their latrines partly remain in the outer wall. An outer bawn extended 30m towards the bank of the River Maigue, where a much altered range of buildings still remain in a roofed but empty condition. Gerald FitzMaurice built a castle here soon after obtaining the manor c1200. It was repaired in 1334 by John Darcy but most of the remains probably date from the 15th century, when Croom was held by FitzMaurice's descendants the earls of Kildare. They lost it after the rebellion of 1534. Edward Perry was besieged here in 1641 by William Leo.

COURT   R475526

This U-shaped tower measuring 8m by 6.6m with a staircase and latrine on one side looks as if it may once have formed part of a twin-towered gatehouse. It was held by Garry MacGibbon MacRenold in 1583, and in 1702 belonged to Henry Widenham.

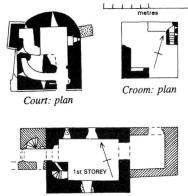

Court: plan

Croom: plan

Plan of Clonshire Castle

Court Castle

CULLAM   R475520

Only the north end wall containing staircases remains of this 7.6m wide tower. There were two upper levels over a vaulted basement. It was battered into submission by Sir Hardress Waller in 1651, lay ruinous in 1655, and was probably never restored. See page 98.

DUNNAMAN   R472421

There is a sheela-na-gig on the east wall of this tower measuring 14m by 10.3m built by the Thorntons in the late 16th century. This wall contains a wide spiral stair in the SE corner and two mural chambers over the entrance passage. The second storey main room is vaulted. The third storey has a fireplace at the east end of the north wall.

DYSERT   R286505   D

Jason Gould held this 14.5m high tower at his death in 1600. Measuring 9.1m by 6.8m and having a projection with a latrine-chute at the west end of the south wall, it contains a barrel-vaulted cellar with three double-splayed loops, two further levels under a pointed vault, and a thinly walled fourth storey which is arched over at the west end. The second storey has a latrine in the SE corner and a mural room with a machicolation covering the entrance.

Dysert: plans & section

0   10

metres

Dunnaman Castle

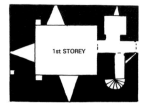

Plans of Dunnaman Castle

Dysert Castle

Fanningstown Castle

FANNINGSTOWN   R499442   D

Towers about 6m square survive at the SW and SE corners of a bawn now occupied by farmbuildings. Each had a third storey level bartizan on the outermost corner, and a spiral stair in a turret projecting from the corner within the bawn. The SE tower remains complete as part of a farmhouse, but only the stair turret and bartizan corbels remain of the upper part of the SW tower. The castle was granted to Sir Henry Wallop in 1592, and to the Fannings family in 1655.

Clonshire Castle

Window at Dunnaman

Fantstown Castle

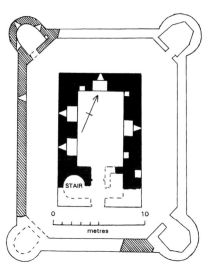

Plan of Garraunboy Castle

FANTSTOWN   R649279   C

This 17m high 16th century tower measuring 13m by 8.6m had a cellar and a loft under a barrel-vault, three upper storeys and an attic within the lost parapet. The third and fourth storeys have fireplaces in side-walls, and the fifth storey has a fireplace in the SW end wall. There are bartizans containing rooms opening off the fourth storey on the NW and SE corners and there are corbels for a machicolation over the entrance in the NE wall. An arch over this end of the lowest level carries a passage leading from the spiral stair in the north corner round behind a room with gunloops to a latrine in the SE wall. The castle was held in 1583 by Jason ffant, and had probably then recently been erected by him. It was held jointly in 1666 by Captain Ponsonby and Lord Colloony.

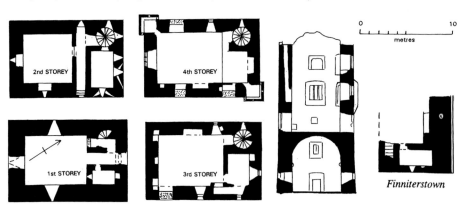

Plans & section of Fantstown Castle

Finniterstown

Glebe Castle

Garraunboy Castle

Fireplace at Fantstown

FINNITERSTOWN   R443424   D

The east and south walls stand four storeys high, the south wall having a mural chamber in its base and a three light window higher up, whilst the east wall contained a chamber at second storey level and a latrine in the SE corner. Once held by the Finniters, the castle passed from the Earl of Kildare to Edward Fitzgerald in 1572. It was ruined by 1655.

GARRAUNBOY   R436444   D

The outer wall of the thick end wall of a five storey tower 14m long by 9m wide has fallen although the rest still stands high, with a vault over the fourth storey. Closely surrounding the tower are remains of a small rectangular bawn with four D-shaped flankers between 4m and 5m in external diameter. One still retains a vault and three gunloops. Hugh Wall held the castle in 1583, but the Stephensons of Dunmoylin held it from 1615 until the Cromwellian confiscations of 1655.

Finniterstown Castle

GLEBE   R356411   D

There are no vaults in this four storey 12m high tower with walls 1.8m thick lying behind a house just west of Rathkeale. There are parapets on the east and west walls but gables with chimneystacks rise directly off the outer edges of the north and south end walls.

GLENOGRA   R591418   D

Of a castle built c1400-18 by Thomas, 6th Earl of Desmond there remains a massive octagonal tower 13m in diameter with a dome-vault and staircases following the line of the outer wall. There is also the lower part of a wall 3m thick connecting it to the base of a second tower which is a semi-octagon. The original bawn would have been about 40m square and may have been copied from the Staffords' castle at Newport in South Wales which has octagonal corner towers on the river front. A thinner wall of late 16th date has replaced the original wall on the south and east sides and extends the enclosure another 20m to the west. It has a plain pointed gateway arch on the south side. The castle was ruinous when forfeited in 1583. It was later granted to the Bourchiers, later earls of Bath.

GLENQUIN   R246264   B

This tower measuring 12.6m by 9.2m was probably built in the early 16th century by the O'Hallinans, who were shortly afterwards almost wiped out by the O'Briens. It was surrendered to the English in 1569 and granted firstly in 1587 to Captain Hungerford and then in 1599 to Captain Collum of Glengoume. In the 1840s it was restored for use by the Duke of Devonshire's agent and more recently it has been repaired as a state monument, several windows having been replaced or patched up. The second and fourth of the six storeys are vaulted, and the hall on the fifth storey has two-light windows. The east corner containing the staircase rising up higher as a turret. Beside it is a NE facing entrance surmounted by a tier of small rooms, and there are latrines in the north corner.

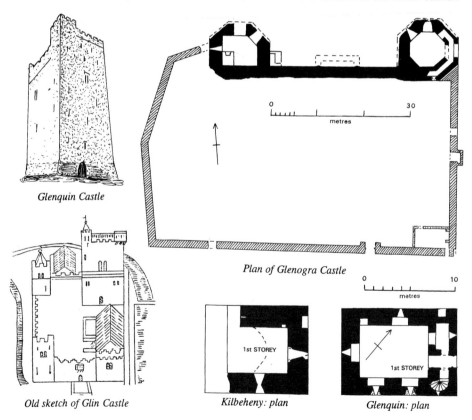

Glenquin Castle

Plan of Glenogra Castle

Old sketch of Glin Castle

Kilbeheny: plan

Glenquin: plan

Gateway at Glenogra Castle

GLIN R130475   C

This tower now stands 12m high but originally it probably stood to 18m with vaults over two of the four storeys. A spiral staircase survives in the NE corner. An old sketch shows the tower standing in one corner of a bawn (which measured 30m by 28m) with square towers at the other corners. This was the main seat of the Knights of Glin, a branch of the Munster Geraldines who held land here for seven centuries and later built a new mansion closeby. One of them was killed defending the castle against Sir George Carew in 1600.

KILBEHENY R847166

This five storey Desmond tower captured by Cromwell in 1650 measures 11.1 by 9.3m. It has a two-light angle loop at the fourth storey level with the mullion forming the corner of the tower. The destroyed end wall probably contained the stair up from the entrance, which has a drawbar slot and faces NW. One of the two loops in the vaulted cellar is double-splayed, with evidence of iron stanchions.

Glin Castle

King John's Castle, Kilmallock

Kilduff Castle

KILDUFF   R777459   C

Moriery Mergagh is said to have had a tower here in 1583, when he was killed during the Desmond rebellion. If this refers to the present building it must have then been newly erected. Parts of a tower about 14m long by 10.6m long stand to full height with evidence of four storeys of unvaulted rooms and an attic with windows in gables surmounted by chimney stacks on both the west and south walls. Only the corners had open wall-walks, with a circular bartizan on pyramidal corners at the NW corner. A very damaged square bartizan on the SW corner contained a roof at third storey level. There was a spiral stair in the SE corner and a tier of subsidiary rooms in the east wall. The Hurleys held Kilduff from 1617 until the 1650s, and in 1667 it passed to the trustees of Erasmus Smith's charity schools, from whom it would have been held by tenants.

KILFINNY   R462399

This MacEniry castle was granted to the Billingsleys in 1588. Lady Dowdall was here besieged for forty weeks by Eady Lacy for the Confederate Irish in 1641. It has a bawn with flankers 4.2m square on the east corners. A 17th century range adjoins the SE flanker. On the west side is a 13th century hall house measuring 16.8m by 8.2m wide over walls 1m thick above a battered base and probably originally having an upper storey hall with a chamber at the north end, where there is straight service stair in a thick end wall. This part was later divided off by an inserted crosswall and built up as a tower with the second level vaulted whilst the hall was given a solid floor over two vaults supported on a longitudinal crosswall and some sort of porch was added at the south end.

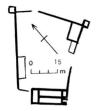

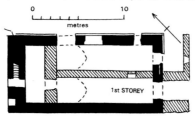

Plans of Kilfinny Castle

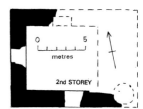

Kilduff: plan

Kilfinny Castle

Knockainy Castle

KILMALLOCK   R608275   B

Part of the basement of the four storey tower called King John's Castle is now a public passageway. Probably of the 15th century, it measures 10.2m by 6.8m and has a straight stair in the east end wall and a turret projecting from the east end of the north wall. It was granted to Henry Billingsley in 1588 and to Thomas Browne in 1604. Lord Castlehaven's forces used the tower as an arsenal in 1645, and in 1651 it was used as a military hospital, whilst in the 19th century it contained a forge and was given large new upper windows. Originally there were several other urban tower houses in the town. Of the 13th and 14th century town walls there remain fragments near the south corner, near which is the Blossom Gate with a small room flanking the east side of a passage 3.5m long and a modest room above. A large bastion was later added near the north end of the long SW side of the town walls, the rest of which was formerly protected by a lake, whilst the River Loobagh flows along the NE side of the town. In 1571 James Fitzmaurice Fitzgerald supported by the Sweeneys and Sheehys captured the English-held town in a surprise night attack and plundered it, taking three days to carry off all the spoils. See p89.

KNOCKAINY   R681359   D

It is uncertain whether the 11m high ruin is the Black Castle held by the earls of Desmond, or the White Castle nearby occupied by their stewards the O'Gradys. Measuring 11.2m by 8m, it has a spiral stair in the NE corner and rooms over the entrance in the east wall. The second storey has a latrine in the SW corner and the fourth storey was a low loft tucked under a vault, above which nothing now survives. Level with the vault a passage off the staircase leads all the way along the north and east walls to a second latrine in the SW corner. An arch over the second storey main room allows the third storey subsidiary room to be almost as large as the main room at that level.

0   10
L_____J metres

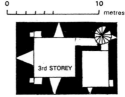

Plans and section of Knockainy Castle

Remains of hall at Limerick Castle

Knocklong Castle

KNOCKLONG   R724309   D

This O'Hurley tower measuring 10m by 9.3m lying in an elevated position on a hillside was held by Garrett MacThomas in 1583. Now badly defaced, but retaining one two light window on the NW side, it seems to have been remodelled in the 17th century, when the existing gables were put on, the vaults over two levels were removed and the floor level of the cellar probably lowered by quarrying away the rock platform.

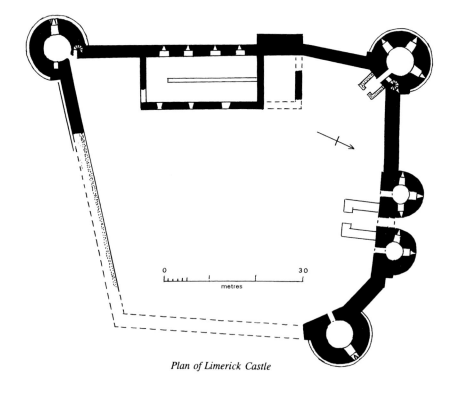

Plan of Limerick Castle

LIMERICK   R577578   E

Limerick was the main seat of the O'Briens descended from Brian Boru until captured in 1194 by Raymond le Gros. Excavations have revealed traces of an earlier fortification beneath the rectangular walled court 66m by 54m erected beside the River Shannon by King John c1210-16. It has circular corner towers up to 14m in diameter, although in the 17th century the towers were reduced in height and given upper vaults to carry cannon. The towerless SE corner was then given an angled bastion, now mostly removed along with much of the adjacent sections of wall, and replaced by an ultra-modern looking museum building. On the north side is a gateway flanked by circular towers 8.5m in diameter. Little remains of a square inner part containing a room from which the portcullis closing the passage was operated. At second storey level the east tower has a window, an arrowloop and a spiral stair leading up, whilst the western tower has two arrowloops and an oddly located doorway (set over a squinch arch) out to the wall-walk. A small rectangular tower adjoins the river front, beside which are the lower parts of a hall and solar. The castle was surrendered to the O'Briens and MacNamaras in 1369 but was recovered soon afterwards and held for the Crown by the citizens of the town.

The castle lay on the west side of the original city (Englishtown), which was walled by the 13th century. The suburb of Irishtown south of Ball's Bridge was given a separate circuit of walls in the early 14th century and in Elizabethan times a citadel was built at the SE end of this with a bastion covering the adjacent St John's Gate. In the Englishtown are remains of two semi-fortified houses built in the early 17th century by the Fanning and Burke families respectively. The latter has a series of bold machicolations, more decorative than functional. Originally there were several other such houses in the city.

Limerick defied Cromwell for a year and a siege begun in 1650 only ended when traitors opened the St John's Gate. In 1690 William III arrived at Limerick but Patrick Sarsfield captured and destroyed his siege train at Ballyneety and he was unable to start a full siege until fresh artillery arrived. The wall was breached near St John's Gate but an attempt to storm the breach was driven back with heavy losses and after a month the siege was raised. Limerick only fell to the Williamites the following year, and the castle only yielded after a heavy bombardment. The city defences were dismantled after it was officially proclaimed that Limerick would cease to be a walled city in 1760.

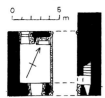

Kilmallock: plan

Kilmallock Gateway

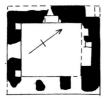

Knocklong: plan

Interior of gatehouse at Limerick Castle

Lissamota Castle

Maidstown Castle

LISMAKEERY   R326476   D

Most of the vault over the second storey has survived the loss of the NE corner and the removal of the upper levels reached by a straight stair in the east wall from the south-facing entrance. There may have been a projection at the NW corner.

LISNACULLIA   R321423   D

The MacSheehies are said to have erected this castle c1460-80. It has a main block measuring 13.9m by 9.3m with walls 1.5m thick above a battered base set on a cliff edge The fireplaces in the west wall of the lowest two levels under a vault are insertions. Above there was just one lofty room. This too had a fireplace in the west wall but it was destroyed in the 1960s when the wall above collapsed. The wing clasping the SE corner contains a newel-stair reached from the main block by an awkward zig-zag passage, although there is no certain evidence of the wing being an addition. Two upper levels are reached from the main block by a second stair carried on a squinch arch over the northern re-entrant angle. There are fragments of a polygonal bawn measuring about 30m across with an outbuilding and square tower at the corner furthest from the main tower. The castle was confiscated after the 1579 Desmond rebellion and given to Thomas Caune. In 1620 it went to Donogh O'Brien, and in 1655 it was held by Sir Edward Fitzgerald.

Lismakeery: plan

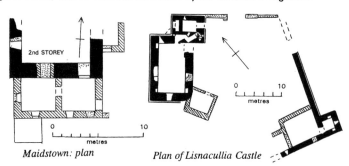

Maidstown: plan

Plan of Lisnacullia Castle

Plans of Lissamota Castle

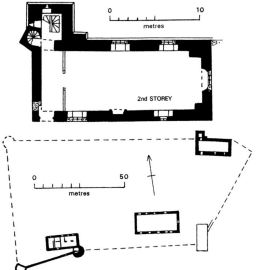

LISSAMOTA   R419388   D

Parapet at Lissamota

Measuring 8.4m by 6.8m, this tower in a farmyard has a thick east wall containing small chambers with latrines over an entrance passage. This part rises above the fairly well preserved wall-walk and parapet and there is a still higher turret over the spiral stair in the SE corner. There are four storeys, the upper two above a vault having fireplaces, and there was an attic in the roof. The castle was granted to the Billingsleys in 1588 but in 1599 was captured by the former owners, the de Lacys.

MAIDSTOWN or BALLYVENOGE   R584320

Only the southern half now remains of a tower which probably measures about 10m by 9m. South of it lies a thinly walled four storey extension of c1600-40, now propped up by a sloping SW corner buttress. It has a blocked entrance and several hood-moulded windows, also mostly blocked up. Very little now remains of a further extension to the east towards where a modern house now stands. It contained a wide new staircase. Maidstown was held in 1660 by Captain Ormsby and later passed to the Gubbins family.

NEWCASTLE CLANWILLIAM   R610573

This 15m high tower has large upper windows and gables surmounted by chimney stacks. The west wall and a projecting turret collapsed c1800, probably undermined by quarrying away of the rock upon which the castle is built. Newcastle was held by William Bourke in 1583, and by Jordan Roche from 1623 until 1655.

Plans of Newcastle West Castle

Newcastle Clanwilliam Castle

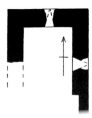

Portrinard: plan

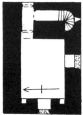

Chapel converted to hall block at Newcastle West

Oola: plan

NEWCASTLE WEST   R279336   E

A 15th century block containing two levels of main chambers, but with a tower rising three more storeys at the west end adjoins a house in private grounds. A 16th century circular tower about 7m in diameter adjoins the SE corner and has a 25m long length of curtain wall running west from it to another tower. Further east is a block 24m long by 11m wide externally with fine 14th century two-light windows on the south side. The arrangement of the features suggests it was a chapel. To the NE of this lies a hall-block 9m wide created later out of a 13th century chapel, the stumps of lancets of that period still remaining on the south side and at the east end. In a mid-15th century remodelling by James, 7th Earl of Desmond, a turret was added at the NW corner and a vault inserted to carry the floor of the new hall. This part has recently been opened to the public after being drastically restored by the Office of Public Works. Its lower level contains a fireplace dated 1635 brought in from a castle near Kilmallock and bearing initials of members of the Herbert or Hawell family. Confiscated after the fall of the Desmond FitzGeralds, Newcastle was granted in 1591 to Sir William Courtenay. It was captured by the Sugan Earl of Desmond in 1598 but recaptured by the English in 1599. After a four month siege by the Confederate Catholics the castle was surrendered in June 1643 and then burnt.

OOLA   R836419   C

This four-gabled late 16th century O'Brien tower with circular bartizans on the NE and SW corners measures 11.8m by 8.6m. The end has a tier of rooms over the blocked entrance and there is a spiral staircase in the SE corner. The upper three levels have two-light windows with hoodmoulds and fireplaces in the east and west end walls.

PORTRINARD   R102283

Much obscured by vegetation and ivy, and difficult of access, is the north end of a tower 9m wide. Part of a vault remains over the second storey and two fragmentary storeys above it. In 1418 Thomas, 6th Earl of Desmond was banished for marrying his tenant Catherine MacCormack, whom he had fallen for whilst out hunting from this castle.

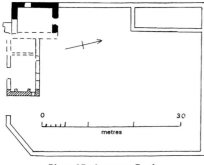

Plan of Rathcannon Castle

Rathnasaer Castle

RATHCANNON   R580345   D

Footings of a wall 1m thick enclose a bawn 40m by 30m with a low cliff below the east side, where a higher fragment remains at the chamfered-off SW corner. Footings of a building lie in the NW corner, and at the SW corner is a fragmentary tower house 10m by 7.8m with evidence of a former vault over the third storey. Adjoining the destroyed east side of the tower was a later wing, now represented by footings and its end gable with fireplaces on two levels. This Casey seat, originally a possession of the earls of Kildare, passed by marriage to Sir Drury Wray but in 1624 was held by Sir William Parson.

RATHMORE   R566414

This tower measuring 10.7m by 8.8m has five storeys with a vault over the fourth level. A thick end wall contains a latrine at ground level, five upper chambers, and a sixth chamber with its inner wall carried on an arch over one end of the topmost principal chamber. In 1580 this Desmond castle was captured by Sir Nicholas Malby, Governor of Connacht, after his nearby victory over Sir John Desmond and the Papal Legate Saunders.

RATHNASAER   R375393   D

This Desmond tower measuring 8.6m by 7.2m has two storeys below a vault and one more above, all the levels being rather defaced. The SE corner contains a spiral staircase and the east wall contains two rooms over the entrance passage. A lost upper storey had a latrine in the NE corner. Rathnaser was granted to the Billingsleys in 1588. Here in 1599 the O'Neill Earl of Tyrone proclaimed James FitzGerald as Earl of Desmond.

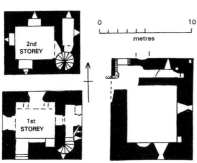
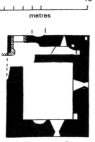

Rathnasaer: plans   *Rathmore: plan*   *Rathcannon Castle*

RATHURD　R595540

This 10.5m high circular tower adjoining a farmhouse contains four storeys of rooms 6m square with the third level vaulted. It was occupied by the Brownes in 1583 but by 1600 had passed to Nicholas Stritch, and in 1646 it was granted to Captain Friend.

ROBERTSTOWN　R270501　D

This Desmond tower measuring about 11m by 9m was later held by the MacClanchys. Fragments of its northern corners lie beside a tidal creek. Further south are low featureless remains of a bawn wall closing off the neck of the promontory. See p98.

ROCKSTOWN　R623423　D

On a commanding rock outcrop a five storey tower measuring 12.2m by 8.8m over walls 2m thick stands 16.4m high to the wall-walk. The parapet has gone and only corbels remain of a machicolation covering the entrance in the south wall, above which are three levels of mural chambers, all vaulted except for that at third storey level. The spiral stair in the SE corner has two angle loops and the second storey main room, which is vaulted, has two more in the NE and NW corners. The third storey had windows of two lights facing north and west and there is a fireplace in the angle between them. There was access off the stair to latrines in the east wall at the second and fourth levels. The thinly walled fifth storey over a second vault had two-light windows on three sides.

Shanpallas Castle

Rathurd Castle

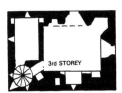
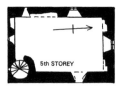
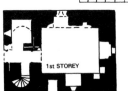
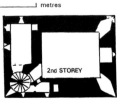

Plans & section of Rockstown Castle

Robertstown Castle

Shanid Castle

Rockstown Castle

SHANID R242451 D

Low, defaced fragments remain of a shell wall 1.5m thick around an oval court on a
natural mound 11m high with a bailey 40m by 30m extending down a slope to the NE.
The east side of the shell wall stood nearly complete a century ago. Inside it about a third
of a tower keep stands complete to the wall-walk. Circular inside but multi-sided outside
(although without proper quoins), and measuring 12.6m in diameter, the keep contained
just one upper room over a basement. Probably built c1200-10 by Thomas Fitz-Maurice,
Shanid was briefly the chief seat of the Desmond FitzGeralds but was later eclipsed by
seats at Askeaton, Newcastle and Trallee. It was captured by Hugh O'Donnell in 1601.

SHANPALLAS R431549 D

On a rock beside a stream is the northern half of an 18m high tower measuring about
10.5m by 9m. The second of the five storeys was vaulted. The round turret with a
staircase nearby is a relic of a bawn 18m square, now partly filled with farmbuildings. This
castle of the earls of Desmond was captured by Sir Henry Waller for Cromwell in 1650.

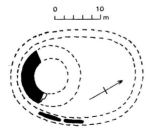

Plan of Shanid Castle

Shanid Castle

Springfield Castle

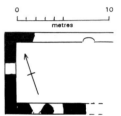

Tooreen: plan

Interior of Tomdeeley Castle

SPRINGFIELD   R349227

The roofless but well preserved late 16th century tower has four gables rising direct off the outer walls, and two circular bartizans at diagonally opposite corners. The second of the four storeys is vaulted. A circular bawn flanker lies closely. Here in 1579 the Earl of Desmond's brother John inflicted a severe defeat on an English force. After Sir John Fitzgerald fled to France following the Treaty of Limerick in 1691 Springfield went to the FitzMaurices and later passed to the Deanes, Lords Muskerry. They laid out a new house in the bawn, but it was replaced after being burnt in the Civil War of 1923.

TOMDEELEY   R324520

Close to a medieval church lies a hall-house built by a 13th century bishop of Limerick. It measures 20.6m by 10.6m over walls 1.1m thick above a deeply battered base. the lowest level has five damaged loops and an entrance facing south and there was probably another doorway above (now a ragged hole), but there is also a modest upper doorway facing north. The upper level has four wide embrasures for former two-light windows and the thicker west end contains a latrine and staircase up to the wall-walk, now lacking its parapet. The castle later passed to the Desmond FitzGeralds. There is no evidence that they remodelled any of the windows but the timber floor of the hall was replaced by a pair of vaults supported upon a central longitudinal arcade of six low arches. The arcade and vaults have survived the loss of the central pier. Thick walls containing a stair leading up divide off the west end of the lowest level, suggesting that there was an intention to make this end into a tower rising above the rest of the building.

TOOREEN or CARRIGPARSON   R631534

The west end remains of a house 8.8m wide and over 14m long over walls 1.1m thick. It may date from after 1622, when a ruinous Riordan castle here was granted to Sir William Parsons. There are openings for windows but no features survive of any interest.

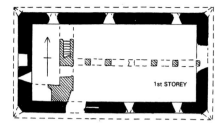

Plans & section of Tomdeeley Castle

TULLOVIN   R536389   D

This building with finely worked openings and a sheela-na-gig on the SE corner is only the end wall of an intended tower. Measuring 9.6m by 5.4m, it contains a spiral staircase and two levels of chambers over an entrance passage flanked by a guardroom. Off the passage from the stair to the third storey of the never constructed main part of the tower is a doorway to a latrine in the south wall. The property passed in the early 17th century from the Leos family to the Parsons family.

Tullovin: plan

WILLIAMSTOWN   R614470   C

There is a circular bartizan with gunloops on the SW corner of this tower measuring 9m long by about 7.5m wide lying beside a road, and there is a turret over the staircase in the NW corner. The bartizan and parapet were repaired in the 19th century, when a number of other alterations were made. The fifth storey has two-light windows in the north and south end walls.

Tullovin Castle

Williamstown Castle

OTHER CASTLES IN COUNTY LIMERICK

BALLYCULLEN R321491 House of c1740 has thick-walled lowest level with battered base which may be a relic of a fortified house of the Nash family.

BALLYNAMONA R691385 Fallen fragment of walling 1.4m thick from corner of tower in field to north of overgrown cemetery.

BALLYNOE R352325 Thinly walled tower 10m by 6.5m.in farmyard. Two somewhat altered levels remain under a vault.

BLACK CASTLE R628405 & KNOCKFENNELL R639407 See Bourchiers entry, page 67.

CARRIGANLEA R410540 Fragment of tower of Knights of Glin on 9m high rock. Held by Thomas Fitzgerald in 1655. Now inaccessible due to dense vegetation.

CLOGH EAST R394439 Slight remains of east side of building and fragments of a wing added beyond it. The castle was granted to James Stroude in 1587. See p63.

CORGRIG R255510 Lower part of tower 3m high on a low rock by stream. Now totally obscured by vegetation. Granted to William Trenchard 1587.

CREGGANE R533258 Lowered and given a new roof in 1840, and now reduced to the SE and SW walls with two loops and evidence of second storey vaulting.

DROMBANY R608519 Tall ruin totally obscured by ivy and surrounding vegetation.

GRANGE R628406 Base of tower 12m by 9m over walls 2m thick on rock. Held by the Earl of Bath in 1655.

HERTBERTSTOWN R687415 Just the footings of the west wall remain beside a farm.

KILCULLANE R672398 Low fragment of corner and buried footings near river.

KILFINANE R681232 Three storey SW end of tower in yard beside road. Counterscarp banks around motte rising 10m to summit 15m across on high ground SW of village.

KILLEEDY R270263 Four storey high west corner fragment of tower on mound by stream. Ditched platform to NE may contain vaults. Held by Earl of Desmond in 1581.

KNOCKATANCASHLANE R681501 Lower part of wall on accessible west side of bawn. Other sides now quarried away into sheer cliff.

LICKADOON R602506 Defaced north wall of O'Hurley tower two storeys high with traces of NE corner staircase. One fine window head loose on ground beside it.

LUDDENMORE R641480 Fragment of NE corner of Bourke tower later held by the Goulds.

RATH R726525 Fragment of bawn wall forms part of yard of derelict farmhouse.

RAWLEYSTOWN R653427 Thin featureless bawn walls of uncertain date plus lower part of thicker north wall. A Rawley seat described as ruinous in 1655.

Cullam: plan

Robertstown: plan

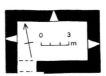
Ballynoe: plan

Creggane: plan

Ballynoe Castle

Loose window-head at Lickadoon

CASTLE SITES IN COUNTY LIMERICK

AUGHINISH R285532 Site of building measuring 19.5m by 8.3m by industrial complex. Held by Teige O'Donogh in 1584.

BAGGOTSTOWN WEST R661339 Site of tower with bartizans on main block and NE turret and 1619 datestone. Held by the Baggots until Cromwellian times.

BALLYGUILEATAGGLE R460328 Base of tower may survive under modern building.

BALLYMACSHANEBOY R592206 An arch still remained in 1840.

BALLYNEETY R782405 Footings on rock visible a century ago. Held by Whites. A ruin in 1690 when Sarsfield destroyed William III's artillery-train nearby.

BALLYSTEEN R341546 Site. Ruined by 1655. Sold in 1703 to Westropp family.

BRUFF R326360 Tower 10m by 5.7m (probably a thick end wall), and 7m high destroyed in late 19th century. Held by the Lacys, Harts, and Tonges in turn.

CARRIGKITTLE R743401 Footings of tower on rock still visible a century ago.

CASTLE ERKIN R707489 Only earthworks now remain on the site of this building.

CASTLE MUNGRET R538544 Vaulted basement remained in 1840.

CASTLE ROBERTS R483438 A ruin in 1595. Granted to Wallop family. Castle and church both demolished for materials to build a bridge.

CLOGHNAROLD R344418 A fragment still stood near church in 1840.

DERREEN R420524 End walls of building 15m by 6m still survived a while ago.

GORMANSTOWN R663325 A thick end wall seems to have survived until fairly recently. The castle was described as decayed in 1655, when held by Edward Fox.

INCH ST LAWRENCE R653497 Site of castle of the Burkes of Brittas.

KILMACOW R463380 Site of tower and bawn held by the Supples as tenants of the earls of Desmond.

LONGFORD R844448 Fragment of O'Brien tower still stood 6m high a century ago.

MILLTOWN R341471 Small low pile of debris on site of tower.

MUSKRYNOONAN or GARDENFIELD R387232 Site of castle of O'Noonan family.

PULLAGH R501372 Site of tower said to have measured 11.5m by 8m.

RATHKEALE Site of Desmond castle burnt by Sir Nicholas Malby after his victory at Monasternenagh in 1580 and held by Maurice MacEdward Hubbert in 1586.

TULLABRACKY R630381 Destroyed in 1810 but parts may survive in stables.

WOODSTOCK R420373 Lacy tower still stood 11m high with walls 1.7m thick about a century ago.

OTHER CASTLE SITES: Abington R715535, Annaghrosty R548501, Ashill or Castle Coote R605273, Ballynacourty R711182, Ballygarde R616481, Ballynahinch R707280, Ballyclogh R311484, Ballyclough R577523, Ballyduff R792211, Ballygrennan R560598, Ballynanty or Moylish R561587, Ballynash R331532, Ballytrasna R742453, Ballynarooga R399337, Brickfield R601226, Bulgadenhall R643310, Caherconlish R675488, Caherelly East R669442, Caherguillamore R613396, Cappaculleen R736569, Castle Cluggin R803438, Castle Creagh R788288, Castle Farm R707378, Castle Grey R420520, R538544 Castle Oliver R670200, Castle Quarter R597441, Cloghatacka R484521, Clogh East R394440, Clonmackin R548569, Clonmackin R550572, Courtbrown R335542, Craigard R283460, Cromwell R735389, Curragh Chase R410490, Drombanny R604528, Drombanny R608519, Dromkeen R727475, Farnane R722545, Garryellan R580461, Glennahaglish R769236, Gortadroma R214432, Gotoon R619273, Hospital R707362, Kilcosgrave R277457, Kilculline R672398, Kilfinnane R681232, Kilballyowen R655365, Knockroe Mason R660476, Leagane 601240, Lisduane R485326, Mayne R354292, Mountblakeney R565254, Nicker R758456, Port R102283, Ryves R749299, Skool R615446, Stonefield R352438, Tullerboy R555361

POSSIBLE CASTLE SITES: Athlacca R555342, Ballinacurra R563550, Caherdavin R549578, Clondrinagh R535584, Coolhenon R626540, Loughill R192501, Rinekirk R449570

WESTROPP lists 200 other castles in Limerick, the locations of which remain uncertain.

CASTLES OF COUNTY TIPPERARY

AGHNAMEADLE   S016774

The original entrance of this MacEgan tower measuring 7.2m by 5.6m faces NE and has a machicolation over it. In a later remodelling the vaulted basement has given a new entrance facing SE, the lower part of the stair in the east corner was blocked up and most of the windows were altered or blocked. An inserted second storey fireplace uses a latrine chute as a flue. There are corbels for a circular bartizan on the south corner.

ANNAGH   R828899   D

The south and west walls remain of a tower measuring 12.8m by 9.4m. At second storey level the staircase in the SE corner has an angle-loop and a long passage to a latrine in the SW corner. The third storey room was vaulted. There was a second passage to a latrine in the southern haunch of the vault, and a chamber on the other side. The room above has remains of three-light windows with hoodmoulds, indicating a 16th century date. The east wall contained a tier of rooms over the entrance. Some of the loops have round or ogival heads. John Hurly held this tower in 1640.

ARCHERSTOWN   S152567

The northern part of a tower and a turret projecting east at the NE corner stand three storeys high in a yard beside a house. The staircase in the turret may have been of wood. The second storey has a cusped ogival-headed loop facing east and a gunloop facing north. The third storey was vaulted. The survey of 1654-6 describes the castle, which was originally known as Rathfarne, as held by the "Irish Papist" James Archer. His ancestors are first mentioned here in 1303-5. When attacked in 1641 by Theobald Purcell the garrison under Major Piesley sallied out but were defeated.

Archerstown Castle

Annagh Castle

Ardfinnan Castle

Annagh: plans

Aghnameadle: plans

2nd STOREY

1st STOREY

0   10
m

Ardfinnan: plans of keep

Ardmayle stronghouse: plans

ARDCRONY   R896871   A

In 1640 Daniell Hogan of Graige held this tower 5.6m wide with a vaulted cellar created within the west end of the nave of a church. It has a staircase in the SE corner, and remains of an oriel window facing south at second storey level. There is a head carved upon the corbels for a former bartizan on the SW corner. The north end is missing.

ARDFINNAN   S082177   D

A ruined 13th century three storey circular keep 11.5m in diameter lies on top of a motte erected by Prince John in 1185. The keep has a hall with a fireplace and three windows over a vaulted basement, the rooms being connected by a spiral stair in a projecting semi-circular turret. The windows of the third storey are later medieval alterations. The castle was garrisoned by Cromwellian troops throughout the 1650s and was rebuilt in the 18th and 19th centuries except for a 15th century tower in the SE corner of a court measuring about 50m by 40m which overlooks a bridge over the River Suir.

Ballagh: plan

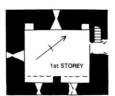

Ardmayle: plans & section of tower house

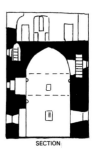

SECTION

0   10
⌞ ⌞ ⌞ ⌞ ⌞ ⌞ ⌟ m

ARDMAYLE   S057458 & 053460

Ardmayle was a Butler seat and has a motte at S058462, a medieval church still in use with an embattled residential west tower, a tower house opposite the church, and a stronghouse down near the river. The 13m high tower house measures 11.2m by 9.2m and has a double-splayed loops in the basement, which has an arcade of two arches on the SE side. Straight stairs in the NW wall rise from the broken entrance doorway facing NE to link three upper levels, the topmost being over a vault with a chamber in its SE haunch. Tucked under the top part of the stair is a latrine in the south corner.

The stronghouse lies within an unfortified bawn of late date. The 18m long north wall still stands four storeys high with three upper levels of mullion-and-transom windows of three lights piercing walling 0.9m thick, but nothing remains of the south side. Square bartizans on pyramidal corbels at the NW and NE corners are the only defensive features. The east end wall has part of a gable surmounted by a chimneystack serving NE corner fireplaces on the first and third storeys. See page 101.

BALLAGH   S007476   D

Only the SW corner with corbels for a bartizan and parts of the 1.9m thick adjoining walls with double-splayed basement loops now remain of a tower once about 11m long by 9.5m wide. The third storey lay over a vault and has remains of a two-light window facing south and arcading on the west, above which the wall was corbelled out internally.

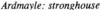

Ardmayle: stronghouse

Ardmayle: tower house

Ballagh Castle

Ballinard Castle

BALLINACLOUGH R984406 D

The lowest two unvaulted storeys containing square rooms still stand 9m high of a 16th century circular tower house 8.2m in diameter. From the north-facing entrance which was set under some sort of recess a stair curves round the east side to the second storey, which has a fireplace on the west and a mural chamber over the entrance. Gunloops open off the staircase. There is a mention of a hall, castle and two chambers here in 1338.

BALLINARD S255364 C

This five storey tower measuring 11.5m by 10m now adjoins an inhabited 19th century house to the west of it. The tower has third storey angle-loops at the NW and SE corners, whilst the fourth storey has an angle-loop at the NE corner and windows with pairs of ogival-headed lights on each side. The south side has chimneystacks for fireplaces and the parapet on the north wall retains one complete double-stepped merlon, but there are now only low flat parapets upon the raised east and west ends of the building. Originally a Roche seat, it passed later to the Lindsays. The "little narrow barbican" mentioned in 1650 may have been a small forecourt like that at Clara in Co Kilkenny.

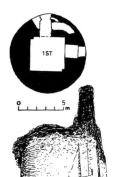

Ballinaclough: plans & view

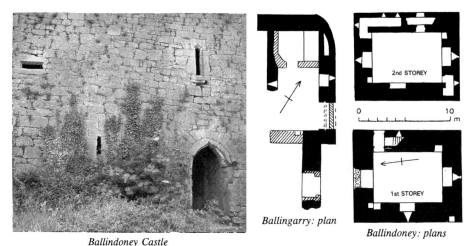

Ballindoney Castle

Ballingarry: plan

Ballindoney: plans

BALLINDONEY   S104206   C

This four storey tower measuring 11.8m by 9.8m with the end walls continued up one stage higher is first mentioned in 1547. The north end wall contains a large fifth storey room with a NE angle loop and a machicolation commanding the entrance doorway on the east side. Communication between the wall-walks on the side walls was by means of steps corbelled out up over the roof. The fourth storey has a two-light window with a hoodmould looking out over the entrance and another in the north end wall. One loop opening off the straight stair in the east wall takes the form of a horizontal slit and at the SE corner the same wall has a crossloop higher up. The second storey has a mural chamber over the entrance and a latrine in the SW corner.

BALLINGARRY   R984957   C

A 6m high wall 2m thick surrounds a bawn 56m by 52m with a gatehouse with a blocked passage with a portcullis groove projecting 1.7m eastwards from the rounded NE corner. The inner parts of the gatehouse are later. The bawn wall contains loops 2m above the internal level. The house on the west and a gateway facing north are late 19th century.

BALLINTOTTY   R913782   D

This four storey round-cornered tower measures 11.7m by 9.2m over walls 2.2m thick. From the entrance in the east wall (where there are gable-marks of a destroyed added range) straight stairs rise in the north and west walls. The second and third storeys have latrines near the SE corner and fireplaces in the east wall. The fourth storey lies over a vault and has an inserted fireplace in a former window embrasure on the west, a window of two ogival-headed lights facing north and three mural chambers. The north and south walls continue up one stage further with the wall-walk continuing through them as passages. At this level the SW corner contains a finely-made cross-loop. Corbels remain of a former bartizan on the SE corner.

A 2m high rampart and 1.5m deep ditch defended the landward side of a promontory enclosure 65m by 50m to the NW at R910784, excavated recently prior to road works. Within was the lower part of a hall house 13.5m by 10m over walls 1.8m thick with a subdivided basement. Henry III coins and pottery suggested a mid 13th century date.

Ballybeg Castle

Ballintotty Castle

Plans of Ballybeg Castle

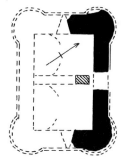

Ballintotty: plan

Ballyboy: plan

BALLYBEG   S180535   C

Of a two storey 17th century house added to the east side of this tower of the earls of Ormond measuring 10.5m by 9.5m over walls 2m thick there remain a gable-mark and a skin of walling pierced by an arch added to carry its upper floor. This wall contains the entrance beside a stair in the north wall. There are vaults over the second and fourth storeys and there are tiers of vaulted passages in the east and west end walls, which rise one stage higher than the rest of the building. The third storey main room has a window of two ogival-headed lights. This level and that below have latrines on the west.

BALLYBOY   S021144

Standing about 4m high is the northern half of a 13th century hall-house 14m long by about 10m wide. The two surviving corners have circular turrets 4m in diameter projecting no more than about 0.7m beyond the main wall. Nothing remains of the southern half and even the ground it stood upon has gone. The basement had a loop at each end and was later divided into two vaulted cellars, the vaults being carried upon an inserted crosswall and the corbels of the former wooden floor of the upper level. A gap on the north wall may represent the remains of an upper floor entrance doorway.

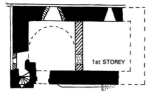

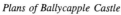

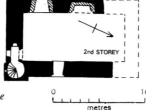

Plans of Ballycapple Castle

Loop at Ballintotty

BALLYCAPPLE　R948865　D

This 9m wide 13th century hall house was later remodelled with an inserted crosswall carrying two plank-centred vaults over the lowest level, a third storey created in the former roof-space, and a new entrance (now blocked) inserted in the south wall. The building was probably just over 14m long but now lacks its north end wall. A window has been formed from the original entrance at second storey level facing east. A wing projecting east at the SE corner containing a spiral stair may be an original feature. The second storey has a fireplace in the west wall with a chimney stack above.

BALLYCOLLITON　R843766　D

Modern outhouses beside an inhabited mansion surround a tower measuring 6.4m by 5.3m with a fireplace in the lowest level. No staircase survives. Above the vault over the third storey there is now a water tank and a modern bellcote.

BALLYDOYLE　S113337　D

Lying within a horse training track is a round-cornered tower measuring 11.5m by 9m set on a low platform. The entrance lies in the west wall. There are three storeys under a vault and a fourth storey on top but the SE corner is destroyed from the third level.

Ballycapple Castle

Ballydoyle Castle

Ballyerk Castle

Ballyfinboy Castle

BALLYDRINAN   S065187

Now reduced to a pile of rubble, this tower measuring 11m by 9.6m above a damaged plinth lacked mural chambers and may have been earlier than neighbouring towers. Two inserted octagonal piers carried an arcade which in turn carried two slightly pointed vaults. It was already ruined by the mid 17th century, when held by Lord Cahir.

BALLYERK   S176666

There is said to be a crosswall within the lowest storey of this tower of the earls of Ormond and that the SW wall contains a latrine chute and fireplace, but the building is now too obscured by fallen rubble and ivy for this to be verified. There are no vaults. Part of the NW wall still stands five storeys high but the rest is much broken down.

BALLYFINBOY   R899936   C

The SE corner of this tower measuring 13.6m by 9.2m bears a sheela-na-gig and contains a spiral staircase. The second storey has a fireplace on the north, a mural chamber in the NW corner, and a latrine with a SW angle-loop reached from the staircase (with another angleloop) by a long passage with three loops south-facing loops. There is another such passage to a latrine level with the vault over the third storey main room. The east wall contains three levels of rooms over the entrance passage and guard room.

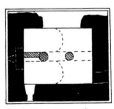

Ballydrinan: plan

Ballycolliton

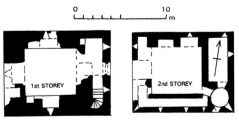

Plans of Ballyfinboy Castle

Bawn gateway at Ballygriffin

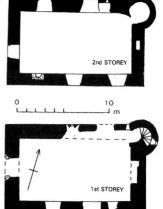

Plans of Ballyglasheen Castle

BALLYGLASHEEN   S278253   C

This late 16th century stronghouse has an entrance covered by a machicolation next to the circular NE corner turret containing a spiral staircase. The corner diagonally opposite has a circular bartizan. There are hoodmoulds over the two-light windows at third storey level and over the single-light windows of the fourth storey partly in the roof with gables rising directly from the end walls, whilst the second storey once had three-light windows. The east wall contains a kitchen fireplace at ground level and there are blocked second and third storey fireplaces in the south wall. The internal plastering shows signs of internal timber dividing walls. On the SW corner are corbels for a former bartizan.

BALLYGRIFFIN   S008404   C

A large bawn with a round-arched gateway facing north and flankers on the NW and SW corners contains a modern house in the SW corner and the western half of a small tower standing to full height with a parapet and evidence of five storeys without vaults. Over the bawn gateway is a recess for an armorial panel or datestone.

BALLYHERBERRY   S136425

A loopholed wall 1.2m thick and 4m high surrounds a bawn about 43m by 41m. There may have been a house or tower in the SW corner, east of which the south wall is reduced to footings. A ruined later house lies in the middle of the east side.

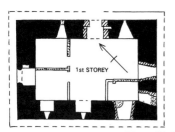

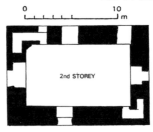

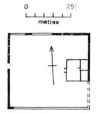

Plans of Ballylusky Castle

Ballyherberry: plan

Ballyglasheen Castle

Ballylusky Castle

BALLYLUSKY   R912885   D

Above a wide and partly defaced battered base this 13th century hall house measures 15.4m by 10.4m. There are corbels for a machicolation over an inserted ground level entrance on the NE side, where there is an original doorway (later converted into a window) further south east on the upper level. This level has a latrine in the north corner and another small room in the south corner. Very little remains of a 17th century house added on the SW side. Described as ruined in the 1650s, the castle was held by Richard Butler of Kilcash in 1640.

BALLYMACADY   R974355

This 16th century tower measuring 14.5m by 11.4m has on each side a gable-shaped recess originally commanded by gunloop in the apex looking down from a cill of a window in the now destroyed third storey. Part of the second storey vault remains but the east end of the building containing chambers over the entrance and a SE corner spiral stair is now reduced to the thin outer wall, the inner walls having been destroyed.

BALLYMACKEY   R943806   D

A crosswall supports two vaults in the basement of this tower measuring 14.7m by 9.4m with an entrance lobby and guardroom in the south wall. There is a straight stair in the east wall. The second and third levels have remains of fireplaces in the south wall. Some of the upper windows have ogival-headed lights with hollow spandrels and hoodmoulds, suggesting a date c1600. The building lies in the middle of a pig farm.

O   5
metres
1st STOREY

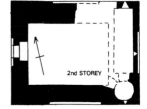

2nd STOREY

Plans & view of Ballymacady Castle

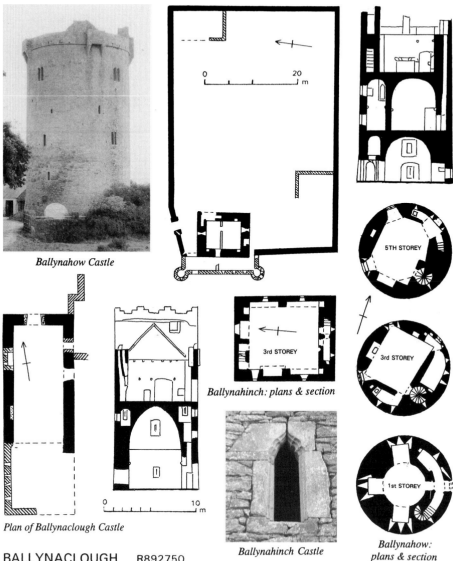

Ballynahow Castle

Ballynahinch: plans & section

Plan of Ballynaclough Castle

Ballynahinch Castle

Ballynahow:
plans & section

BALLYNACLOUGH   R892750

A much altered hall block 7.9m wide lies just SE of a 3m high mound with remains of retaining walls and collapsed fragments. When the ninth Earl of Ormond died in the 16th century there was at the manor of "Weyperous" a hall, a chapel with a thatched roof, and two rooms with a tiled roof. Not much remains of southern extension to what was probably originally a building 15m long. The roll-moulded 13th century window of sandstone in the north wall maybe reset, whilst the west wall has been rebuilt above the lowest level, in which are gunloops, although the lower part of a corbelled chimneybreast also survives. The east wall was mostly rebuilt in the late 17th century when a wing, now very ruined, was added beyond it. See p170.

Ballynahinch Castle

BALLYNAHINCH   S036407

Near the NW corner of a bawn measuring 55m by 53m above the north side of the Suir is a tower measuring 11.4m by 9.4m with its north end wall raised up one further storey to a height of almost 20m. The bawn has a corner-loop and gateway just north of the tower. The length of loopholed bawn wall with small vaulted circular casemate flankers west of the tower is an addition probably of c1580-1600. The tower contained three lofty storeys and has chambers in both haunches of the vault over the second level. The east wall contains a straight staircase rising from a broken entrance beside which there was once a sheela-na-gig. The lowest level has one double-splayed loop and an inserted cross-wall. One upper window with an ogival head is very finely moulded. The third storey has a fireplace built into a former window on the west, a latrine on the south and recesses containing windows on the east and west. A stair in the north wall rises to serve the upper chamber there. A fourth storey was later squeezed into the upper part of the third storey and the roof space, a fireplace being inserted on the west side.

BALLYNAHOW   S083602   A

This 16th century circular tower of the Purcells measures 10.8m in diameter and rises 16m to the wall-walk, off which open four regularly spaced machicolations. There are gunloops opening off the jambs of the window embrasures at each of the five storeys. The two lowest levels under a dome vault are circular but the next two levels are quadrangular with embrasures at the corners and mural chambers beside the spiral staircase. The third storey fireplace has a rope-twist roll-moulding over the mantle, whilst the fourth storey has a rebuilt fireplace with a joggled lintel. The fifth storey, above another vault, has a fireplace, a latrine with a crossloop, and three windows of two lights with round or ogival heads. A secret room on the NE is reached from one of these window embrasures. The lower rooms were still being inhabited as a cottage in the 1840s.

Ballynakill Castle

Ballynoran Castle

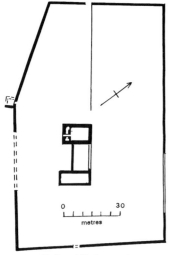

Ballynakill: bawn plan

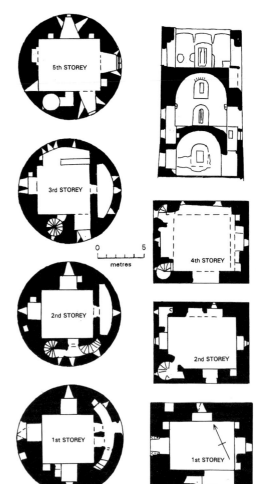

Ballysheeda: plans　　　*Ballynoran: plans & ection*

BALLYNAKILL   SO99855   D

A wall with an external height of up to 7m surrounds a bawn 130m long by 80m wide. There are remains of a turret at a slight angle in the middle of the SW side and a bartizan upon the west corner, whilst there are gateways facing NW and SE, the latter superseded by a later archway just south of it. There are gunloops both at the internal ground level (1m higher than that outside) and in the parapet merlons. In the middle is a much-altered four storey tower house of c1600 measuring 12.8m by 9.5m over walls 1.7m thick, but the SW wall is wider to contain chambers over the entrance lobby and a spiral stair in the west corner. There is recess for a panel with heraldic arms or a date over the destroyed entrance and there are remains of fireplaces at several levels in the SE wall. None of the main rooms was vaulted. A new range was added against the SE side in the late 17th century and in the 18th century a further extension was made and the whole building remodelled, so that the tower only retains original single and two-light windows with hoodmoulds on the NW side. The castle belonged to Richard Butler in 1640.

BALLYNORAN or DUFFHILL   S349229

This Mandeville tower measuring 11.2m by 9.6m has a lofty vaulted basement, two more storeys under another vault and a fourth storey on top with an arcaded east wall, the upper levels being linked by a spiral stair in the SW corner. Another stair in the NW corner then led to the wall-walk, off which was a machicolation over the entrance. There are chambers in the haunches of both vaults. Many of the slabs covering the lower staircase, entrance, and chambers in the badly defaced south wall are missing, and this side is bulging out and in danger of collapse. The second storey has a latrine in the NW corner and a fireplace on the north, whilst the third storey has a SE angle-loop.

BALLYQUIRK   M912022   C

Rubble from the lost upper parts of the east wall blocks the entrance of a chamfered-cornered tower measuring 10.9m by 8.8m which was granted by Thomas, Earl of Ormond in the late 16th century to Bryen O'Kennedy. A stair leads up from the entrance passage. The fireplace in the west wall, the joists remaining over the lowest level and the sash window facing north at third storey level are 19th century, the building having been then used as a cider factory. No original windows survive complete. The third storey is vaulted.

BALLYSHEEDA   R925469   D

This circular tower house 11.8m in diameter was held by Philip O'Dwyer in 1657. It contained five storeys of square rooms with the second level vaulted and there was an attic within the roof. One of the four machicolations at the summit commands the entrance facing SE, above which the next three levels have mural rooms. Other mural rooms (possibly latrines) on the NE now lack their inner walls. The windows of the third and fifth levels had hoodmoulds and are flanked by gunloops. From the entrance a stair curves round to where a spiral stair (now broken) began at second storey level. On the NW a chimneystack rises above fireplaces serving the fourth and fifth storeys.

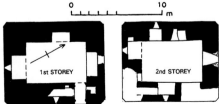

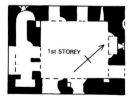

Plans of Ballyquirk Castle   *Ballynakill: tower plan and view of bartizan*

Barrettstown Castle

Ballytarsna Castle before restoration

Plans of Barrettstown Castle

BALLYTARSNA   S116493   C

The 21m high tower of the Hacket family measuring 10.8m by 8.8m lies just north of the SE corner of a bawn measuring about 58m by 45m, and one jamb of the bawn gateway adjoins the tower north wall. Excavations forming part of the ongoing restoration of the tower have shown that the bawn wall was 2.6m thick and earlier than the tower. It had a wall-walk 4.5m above ground and may indeed go back to the late 13th or early 14th century. Currently its partly restored SE corner is visible, together with footings of the rest of the south side and two defaced fragments of the west side. The tower west wall contains a zig-zag entrance passage arrangement with the entrance covered by a crossloop from the basement, which has three restored double-splayed loops. A straight stair rises to a short section of spiral stair in the SW corner, and then another straight stair rises around the west and north sides. There are five storeys with vaults over the second and fourth storeys. The third storey has a latrine in the south end wall, three windows with embrasure seats, and a fireplace with its flue in a projecting breast. The circular bartizans upon the NW and SE corners have just been rebuilt.

BARRETTSTOWN   S183349   D

The third storey of this O'Kearne tower measuring 9.8m by 7.8m has an angle-loops opening off the broken spiral staircase in the west corner, others serving a latrine and another small room in the north and east corners respectively, and a fourth angle-loop opening off one of a tier of rooms over the entrance in the SW end wall. The main room at this level has a fireplace on the SE and a vault, above which is a fourth storey with two-light windows. The second storey also has a fireplace on the SE side.

BAWNMADRUM   S163824   D

A bawn 30m by 26m still has on the north and east sides walls 1.8m thick rising 8m to a wall-walk with a fragmentary parapet, with joist holes of an internal building on the east. Nothing remains of the south wall and only footings remain on the west. The gap in the north wall looks more the result of a weakness caused by latrine passages than a former entrance. There may have been a tower house in the SE corner. The Civil Survey of 1654-6 refers to the bawn as belonging to Thomas Magner of Boolabaun, "Irish Papist".

BEECHWOOD or GRAIGUE UPPER   R911844

The lowest three storeys of a tower originally called Graigue measuring 13m by 9m project from the back of Beechwood House, dating from 1741. The entrance faced south alongside the staircase in the SE corner. A loose window-head is dated 1594 with initials of Oliver Hogan. The second storey has a vault and 18th century sash windows. The third storey has remains of a fireplace on the west and a latrine in the NE corner, while there is a slab-roofed chamber with a tiny entrance hatch within the east wall.

BEHAMORE or HAWKSHAW   R998911

This late tower with gunloops flanking the second storey windows has no vaults. The east wall containing the entrance has fallen. The third storey has a fireplace, a latrine in the SW corner, and two-light windows with hoodmoulds. There is a bartizan on the SW corner and part of a stepped parapet remains on the north side.

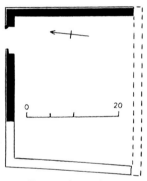

Bawnmadrum: plan

BOOLABAUN   S1556828   D

This tower held by Thomas Magner in the 1650s measures 10m by 8.6m. Now badly cracked, it has a tier of chambers over the entrance passage in the NW wall and remains of a spiral staircase in the north corner. The lofty vaulted third storey has three angle-loops, one of them lighting a latrine in the east corner. Another latrine below is reached by a long passage from the staircase.

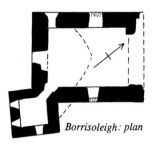

Borrisoleigh: plan

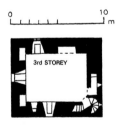

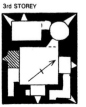
3rd STOREY

2nd STOREY

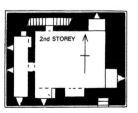

Borris: plans

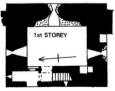

Ballytarsna: plans

Boolabawn: plans

BORRIS: BLACK CASTLE   S193579

The end walls of this tower measuring 13.2m by 10.4m are continued up to contain rooms and serve as gables and there are circular bartizans set on pyramidal corbels at the NE and SW corners. The entrance in the west wall has a zig-zag arrangement of lobbies, allowing a crossloop from the cellar to command the outer doorway. The second and third storeys have mural rooms on the west, fireplaces on the south and straight flights of steps in the north wall. The third storey mural room and a latrine passage in the east wall opening off the stair have angle-loops in the southern corners. A spiral stair in the NE corner leads to a fourth storey hall over a vault with five windows and a chamber in the SE corner. A stair up from the western window embrasure leads to a wall-walk retaining parts of a parapet.

BORRISOLEIGH   S029668   C

A stair turret 5.2m square stands at the south corner of a main block measuring 12.2m by 9.6m, which was much altered in the 18th century when it became a brewery, all the windows being destroyed or enlarged. The turret contains a vault over its third storey and has a squinch arch between it and the main building on the east side. The lowest level has a vault and the drawbar socket of the destroyed entrance facing NE. The fourth storey lies over another vault and has a fireplace in the NE wall. A plaque in the gable of a nearby building is dated 1643 with an inscription referring to Richard Burke and Ellice Hurly.

BUOLICK   S261563   C

To the west of a ringwork (at S263562) measuring about 30m across on top is a tower measuring 11.3m by 9.5m with vaults over the first and third levels, above which nothing remains. A straight stair leads up from an entrance in the west wall. The basement has loops with outer splays and very short cross-slits. The second storey has three window embrasures, remains of a fireplace on the west and a latrine in the north wall. The medieval church to the west has an embattled tower with three upper living rooms (now lacking their east wall) over a vaulted basement. No staircase survives.

Borris: Black Castle

Burncourt Castle

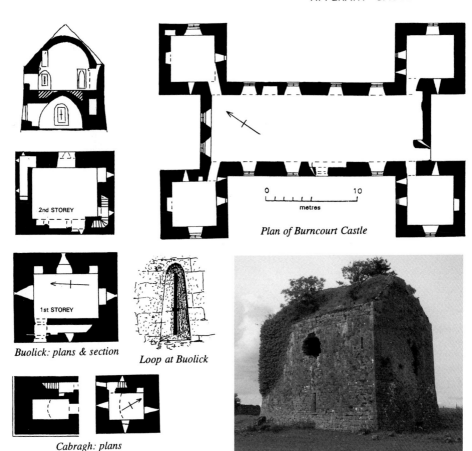

Plan of Burncourt Castle

2nd STOREY

1st STOREY

Buolick: plans & section

Loop at Buolick

Cabragh: plans

Buolick Castle

BURNCOURT   R952181   A

This stronghouse was originally known as Clogheen and the present name refers to its destruction by its owner Sir Richard Everard in 1650 to prevent it being occupied by Cromwellian troops. Sir Richard had only completed the house in 1641 and was hanged by General Ireton in 1651. It was never restored and a print of 1795 shows it as it is now, except that the chimney stacks were then more complete. By then there was a more modest new house at the west end of the bawn and gardens to the north. The ruin has a main block 25m long by 10m wide with a tower 7.5m square at each corner. Both the main entrance in the middle of the west side leading into a service passage at the south end of the main hall, and the back door opening out of the kitchen with a large fireplace at the south end have gunloops in the jambs, and there are several other gunloops. The main block has inverted pyramidal corbels either for a machicolated parapet or a timber-framed gallery, above which are a series of gables with attic windows were raised directly above the outer wall-faces, and the towers given a gable on each of the four sides. Below the hall and kitchen was a very low basement with windows at ground level, and there was a level of state rooms above, bedrooms being provided in the tower, which rise one level higher, i.e. to five storeys including the basement rooms and attics. The upper rooms all have mullion-and-transom windows of two lights.

Cahir Castle

Cahir Castle

CABRAGH   S114557

A thin length of bawn wall lies west of a tower measuring 6.7m by 6.2m. The vaulted cellar has an entrance facing NE. A straight stair in the NW wall leads to a second storey room with three loops and another vault. Nothing remains of the upper levels but old descriptions suggest that there was a bartizan on the north corner. See page 117.

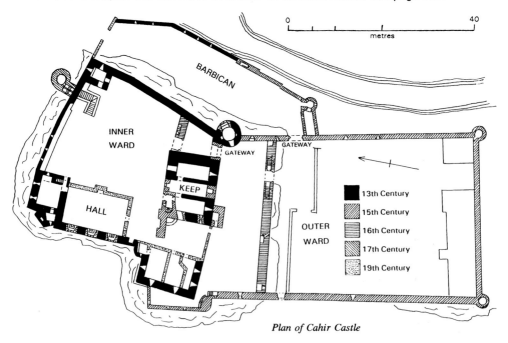

Plan of Cahir Castle

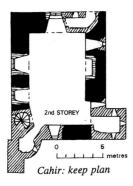

2nd STOREY

0   5
|_|_|_|_|_| metres

Cahir: keep plan

Cahir Castle

CAHIR   S050249   E

Some time during the mid 13th century the Worcester family transferred their main seat from the motte at Knockgraffon to a stone castle built on a rock in the middle of the Suir at Cahir. It has a wall about 1.6m thick and 4m high around a court about 30m square with rectangular towers of differing sizes within the northern corners, a larger tower projecting from the southern half of the west side, a circular tower at the SE corner, and a gatehouse containing narrow guardrooms flanking a vaulted passage and a private hall and main bedroom above. In the early 14th century Cahir passed by marriage to the Berminghams and reverted to the Crown after the execution of Sir William de Birmingham by Justiciar Anthony Lucy in 1332, although in practice the castle and barony had been overrun and devastated by the O'Briens.

In 1375 Cahir was granted to James Butler, 3rd Earl of Ormond and during the 15th and 16th centuries the castle was gradually rebuilt and improved by the descendants of the 3rd Earl's illegitimate son James, who intermarried with the Berminghams and the Desmond Fitzgeralds. The gatehouse was converted into a tower house or keep by blocking up the passage and building a new gateway between it and the SE tower. A spiral stair was inserted in the NW corner, although the foot of it only leads out to the court, not into the lower storey, and a latrine turret was added at the SW corner. An outer ward 60m long by 33m wide with circular turrets at the southern corners was extended to the south, although a strip at the northern end was later divided off in the 16th century to create a middle ward with steps leading up to the wall-walk on either side of its gateway. Just south of here is the main outer gateway on the east side which is enclosed by a barbican of various periods and flanked by a 17th century wing extending out to a circular turret. Also probably 17th century is the circular tower extending out from the inner ward north wall to contain a well. The adjoining NE tower is only entered at second storey level, below which was a prison reached only from above by a trapdoor.

In 1599 the Earl of Essex captured the castle after a three day siege, during which the east wall was breached by cannonfire. Its commander, James, brother of Thomas 2nd Lord Cahir, escaped by swimming under the adjacent water mill and subsequently reoccupied the castle for a while. Prior to the siege the castle was regarded as one of the strongest in Ireland and the temporary defection of its owner was a matter of grave concern for Elizabeth I's government. In 1647 the castle was captured by Lord Inchiquin after a short siege, and it was surrendered to Cromwell in 1650 without a fight. The owners lived nearby during the 18th century and then abroad, but in the 1840s Richard Butler, 13th Baron Cahir, restored the ruined castle, much of the parapets dating from then, along with the inner walls of the SW tower and almost all of the main hall lying between it and the NW tower, which contains two private rooms with latrines in a western turret over a basement with two double-splayed loops. The section of walling with a fireplace adjoining the keep NW corner may mark the position of the kitchen.

CAMUS   S046431   D

Malcolm Hamilton, Archbishop of Cashel died in his castle at Camus in 1629. There are remains of two bawn flankers with battered bases towards the River Suir, and there is a causeway across a former moat on the east side.

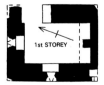

Cappa: plan

CAPPA   R982286   D

The south and west walls of this ruin on a low ridge stand complete to the parapet. The tower measures 10.2m by 8.2m and had barrel-vaults over the second and fourth out of five storeys. From an entrance in the north end of the east wall rose a straight stair in the east wall. The basement has damaged loops facing north and west and deep recesses at the south end. There is a latrine chute at the SW corner. In 1650 it was described as an "old broken castle... irepayreable", and a few years later it was taken from the Bakers and given to the Uniake family, from whom it takes an alternative name of Cappauniac.

CAPPA   R951819

Although retaining part of a gable on the west wall, this is a much defaced five storey tower measuring 7.5m by 6.2m over walls 1.2m thick, part of the cellar vault having fallen, the east entrance being broken out, and the stair in the SE corner being destroyed above the second storey. This level has a NW angle-loop, a latrine in the south wall and gunloops flanking the broken-out west window. The third storey has two blocked gunloops in a niche on the south and a fireplace backed against an east wall containing two levels of small chambers, the uppermost being vaulted. A gable end on this wall suggests a former added range. The castle lay ruinous in the 1650s, when it had a "little barbican".

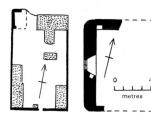

Carney: plans

CARNEYCASTLE   R875899

The 9.5m long west wall of the tower lying in the NW corner of a bawn measuring 44m by 30m still stands four storeys high. The entrance probably lay in the tower south wall. A window in the SW corner has an interlace ring-headed cross carved on the splayed head and there is a head beside the sill of a second storey window. A 19th century house and outbuildings (all of them derelict) also lie within the bawn, which has a round-arched south-facing gateway with decorative terminals.

Carney Castle

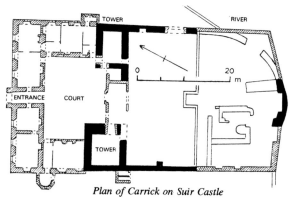

Plan of Carrick on Suir Castle

Two views of Carrick-on-Suir Castle

CARRICK ON SUIR   S405216   E

Edmund Butler is said to have built the first castle on this site beside the Suir in 1309. The alternative name Ormonde Castle refers to the earldom conferred on his son. A D-shaped bawn 30m long with two substantial five storey towers on the vulnerable straight north side, and possibly a third on the south of which little remains, was built in the mid 15th century. The south end of the bawn was later rebuilt to make it more rectangular in shape.

Thomas Butler, 10th Earl of Ormonde, who had been brought up in England and was a courtier of Elizabeth I, added a fine courtyard house of a type more English than Irish against the north side of the castle. It has a long gallery extending along the whole of the north side on the upper storey, there being a bay with a six-light window over a central porch, the other windows being of two lights below and three lights above, all with hoodmoulds. Another bay with a six-light window lying further south on the east side has crossloops piercing the corners at a lower level, the only defensive features of this part of the castle. A chimney breast in the gallery is dated 1565 and there are a fine series of stucco ceilings and wall decorations with heraldry, monograms, mottos and dates. This part is still roofed although the older part is ruined.

In 1649 the castle was surrendered to Cromwell after resisting for just one day after the town was taken. Ormond sent Lord Inchiquin in an unsuccessful attempt to recapture it. It was later granted to Sir John Reynolds but in the 1660s was restored to the 12th Earl. Apart from caretakers the last occupant of the Elizabethan house was a Waterford wine merchant as a tenant in the 1780s. The castle lay at the SE corner of the walled town and protected the east gate just north of it. Fragments of the walls remain between the New Gate on the north side and the NE corner. A map of 1657 suggests there were corner towers. There was also a west gate and a bridge gate near the SW corner.

CARRIGEEN   S196389   D

Within a stud-farm complex (no access is allowed) is a 17th century four storey building with gables surmounted by chimneystacks on the east, south and west walls.

Castle attached to Cashel Cathedral

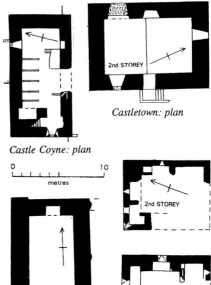

Castletown: plan

Castle Coyne: plan

0   10
|_|_|_|_|_|_|_|_|_|_|
metres

Cashel: plan   *Cashlaunteigeboght: plans*

2nd STOREY

2nd STOREY

1st STOREY

CASHEL   S075409   E

What is now a cathedral close measuring 120m by 90m upon the Rock of Cashel served as a fortress from early times. It was the seat of Brian Boru, crowned High King of Ireland in 977, but in 1101 Muircheartach O'Brien handed it over to the church. Cormac's Chapel was built c1127-34, and the aisleless cruciform cathedral alongside it was gradually erected from east to west during the 13th century. The nave was intended to be longer, but was eventually closed off at the west end by a grim 22m high residential tower, probably by Richard O'Hedigan, Archbishop from 1406 to 1440, who built the Hall of the Vicars Choral on the south side of the close. The tower measures 12.6m by 8.8m and had three storeys below a vault and a hall above approached either by a long flight of steps in the west wall or from a mural passage on the nave north wall. The room and attic above may have been the result of later alterations. The upper parts of the south wall collapsed during a storm in 1847. After the Rock of Cashel was stormed by Lord Inchiquin's forces in 1647 twenty ecclesiastics were killed in the castle after being smothered in fire.

The rock and its buildings lie 60m to the north beyond the town walls thought to have been built by Archbishop FitzJohn in 1317-26. Foundations of a wall 1.8m thick lie on the SE side. The John and Friar gates lay either side of a friary on that side, the Lower Gate faced west, the Canopy Gate faced NE and the Moor Gate faced towards the rock. On the south side of Main Street is Quirk's Castle, a 15th century urban tower house retaining raised NE and SW ends but otherwise much altered.

CASHLAUNTEIGEBOGHT   R838928

Just two storeys remain of the north and east walls of a tower measuring 9.7m by 7.8m over walls 1.8m thick lying on an outcrop. The staircase lay in the lost SW corner and the entrance and mural chambers lay in the south wall. A chamber in the NW corner at second storey level has an angle-loop.

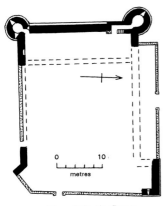

Plan of Castle Grace

Cashlaunteigeboght Castle

CASTLE COYNE   S088276

The thin loopholed west wall survives of a bawn about 25m square. On the north side are a cottage and to the east of it a ruinous building 13m long by 6.8m wide over walls 1.3m thick. One jamb with a loop remains of a doorway on the south side with a drawbar slot. The 3m thick west wall contains a stair rising from a doorway intermediate between the two surviving levels under a vault. A loop in the outer part of the wall opposite this doorway has gunloops on either side.

CASTLE GRACE   S030143

Beside the River Suir are remains of a late 13th century de Bermingham castle with walls 1.4m thick around a court 30m by 23m. The only side which is complete has circular towers 5.5m and 5m respectively in diameter at each end, both being furnished with crossloops. There was an upper floor hall and chamber with windows of one light or two lights with plate tracery along this side. Only a fragment remains of each of the other corner towers, which were square in plan.

Castle Coyne

Castle Grace

Castle Leiny

Castletown Castle

CASTLE LEINY   S148710   D

Only footings remain of a thin wall enclosing a bawn on a rock outcrop. Of a large three storey house there remains only the northern end with a NE turret with small rooms and a staircase rising from the second level. The house once had a turret or wing at the SE corner, making an L-plan. An extra wing was later added to the NW. Held by John Morres in 1640, the house was "without repayre" in 1654-6. See page 168.

CASTLE OTWAY or CLOGHONAN   R945698

A tower house of c1600 originally named Cloghonan measuring 14m by 10.7m over walls 1.2m thick adjoins an 18th century house named Castle Otway, the Otways having been granted the property in 1665. Both parts were remodelled in the 19th century, but the tower retains original windows flanked by gunloops in the NW and NE sides, the latter also having the entrance doorway, off which leads an 18th century staircase.

CASTLETOWN   R734816   C

Held in 1640 by Donogh O'Brien, who may have been its builder, this is a much-altered three storey stronghouse measuring 13.3m by 9.4m beside Lough Derg with the south end still vaulted on the lowest level. The west wall has a tall chimney stack over fireplaces at second and third storey levels and the east wall has a second storey doorway reached by external stairs. In the 19th century a house was added to the SE corner. see page 122.

CASTLETOWN   R822925

This building on a rock beside Lough Derg was restored after the 1650s, when it lay ruinous, and is still occupied. It has 19th century windows and crenellations, plus a SE extension of that period, but retains vaults over three basement rooms, the largest of which was a kitchen with a fireplace in the north wall. The south wall contains the entrance and a straight stair to the second storey. This level and that above have chambers in a triangular spur projecting from the NW corner. The bawn to the south is probably original, but with 19th century battlements, and there is also a walled garden.

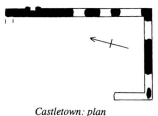

Castletown: plan

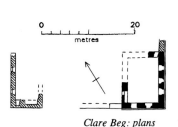

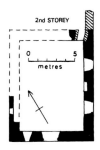

2nd STOREY

Clare Beg: plans

CASTLETOWN   S212636

In 1640 this building above the Black River was occupied by James Butler, but it was "out of repair" in 1654-6. A bawn 29m long by 16m was enclosed by walls up to 1.4m thick now surviving 3m high on the NE, where there are traces of windows and a latrine projection, and, in a more fragmentary state, at the SE end.

CLAREBEG   S255338

Footings remain of the south wall of a bawn connecting a two storey west range with fireplaces in the south end wall and a four storey stronghouse in the SE corner. Little remains of the stronghouse north wall, and nothing at all of the bawn and west range north walls. The stronghouse measures 12m by 9.2m and looks 17th century but may incorporate a 14th century building since an upper fireplace on the west side is built against a trefoil-headed window, an arrangement making it unlikely that the window has been reset. The south and east walls have three levels of mullioned windows over a basement and there is a circular bartizan on the SE corner. The south end gable also remains, with an attic window, and two lower gables upon the east wall. The extension at the NE corner is said to have been a stair turret. In 1650 the castle was occupied by Captain Matthew Jacob, who had recently repaired it.

Castletown Castle

Clare Beg Castle

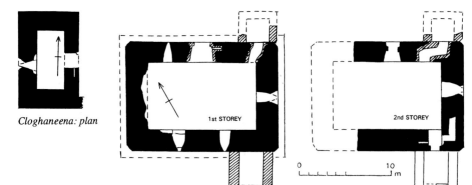

Cloghaneena: plan

1st STOREY

2nd STOREY

0   10
              m

Clohaskin: plans

CLOGHANEENA   R708726   D

The east wall of this tower is thinner than the other sides and seems to have once formed a crosswall between two chambers each about 3m wide. There are no vaults. The remains are much obscured by ivy and no staircase, latrines or fireplaces are now visible.

CLOGHJORDAN   R976882   378

The Cromwellian James Harrison added a two storey T-plan house to the Carrolls' tower house in the 1650s or 60s. The site is surrounded by remains of a wet moat fed by a stream on the west side, although farm buildings have replaced it on the north. The tower measures 9.3m by 8.8m, has a covering of plaster rendering and ivy and lacks original features of interest. The entrance probably faced NE. The tower was lowered in the 19th century to form a wing balancing that then added NW of the 17th century house.

Cloghkeating Castle

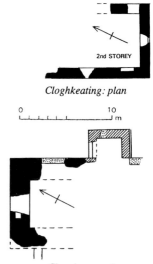

2nd STOREY

Cloghkeating: plan

0   10
             m

Clonakenny: plan

CLOGHKEATING   R935908   C

Corbels carried the upper floor of this hall house 8.2m wide over walls 1.2m thick which was at least 11.2m long, the north end and much of the east wall being missing. The walls rose up higher to enclose the roof and there is no evidence that this roof space was later made habitable. A new ground-level entrance was later inserted in the south wall. The original upper entrance at the SE corner is thought to have had a forebuilding or porch in front of it. Footings of a bawn wall adjoin the SW corner.

CLOHASKIN   S004997   C

The upper level of this chamfered-cornered 13th century hall-house measuring 16.4m by 11.5m over walls 2.2m thick above a defaced battered base has an entrance at the east end of the south wall from which a stair leads up in the east wall. The lower level was later provided with its own entrance facing north and a forebuilding was added in front of the other doorway. The upper room has segmental-arched window embrasures and probably had a latrine in the now very damaged turret projecting north at the NE corner.

CLONAKENNY   S114803   D

One end wall remains four storeys high of a tower 9.6m wide and at least 13m long over walls 2.2m thick. An east projection measuring 4.8m by 3m, perhaps an addition, contains a blocked doorway. A wall up to 1.3m thick enclosed a bawn to the NW, whilst to the south extended a more thinly walled outer bawn of which the 22m long west side remains, with gunloops around the NW corner, and also the 55m long south side. In 1640 John O'Magner held this castle, which was "out of repayre" in 1654-6.

Two views of Clohaskin Castle

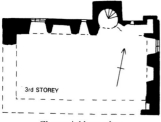

Clonamicklon: plan

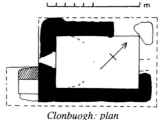

Clonbuogh: plan

Tower at Clonmel

CLONAMICKLON   S282560   D

The Earl of Carrick's youngest son John Butler founded this castle in the early 14th century. The 1.5m thick walling up to 4.5m high surrounding a court 43m square may go back to that period since there are slight remains of a portcullis slot over the gateway on the south side and the nearby SW tower 5.5m in diameter has a crossloop next to a latrine projection against the west curtain wall and a squinch arch joining its second storey to the south curtain wall. Another circular tower, also of three storeys, but slightly smaller and with hoodmoulded windows of much later date, lies at the SE corner, and there was once a domestic range extending between the two towers. Barns fill the east and west sides of the court, which lacks its NE corner. On the north side there remain the north and east walls of a building 18m long by 10.5m wide containing three storeys in the larger southern part and four storeys (within the same height) in the northern part, where there are defaced fireplaces in the east end wall. A spiral stair in a projecting turret on the north served both parts. The mullioned windows with hoodmoulds remaining high up and the east gable with a surmounting chimneystack serving a third storey fireplace all suggest a date possibly as late as 1628, when Sir Pierce Butler was made Viscount Ikerron in 1628. However, the building may be a 14th century hall-keep since the curtain wall of that period abuts against its NW corner and there is a latrine projection high up near the NE corner. The castle was forfeited by the Butlers in 1656 and later leased to the Cooke family.

Clonmel Town Walls

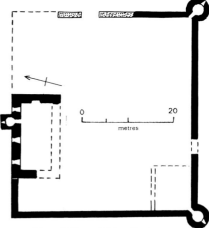

Plan of Clonamicklon Castle

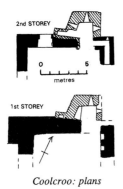

Coolcroo: plans

Clonamicklon Castle

CLONBUOGH   S188744

Only the defaced lowest part remains of a tower measuring about 12.8m by 9.4m over walls 1.8m thick. There are traces of a square turret on the SE corner and the broken down NW corner had a circular turret containing a spiral staircase beside an entrance facing north. The lowest level was vaulted. In the 1650s the then decayed castle was owned by Piers, Viscount Ikerrin.

CLONMEL   S200223   B

The de Grandison lords of Clonmel gradually had the town walled in during the century following a murage grant in 1298. Portions of walling with arcading to support a wall-walk remain around the churchyard in the NW corner where the walls were flanked by four square towers. There are five other fragments further east of the northern walls and the west gate also survives, although it lost its portcullis groove during a rebuilding of 1831. There were four other gates, including two facing the Suir on the south side, and a circular tower at the NE corner. The defences were strengthened with outworks and bastions during the second half of the 17th century.

Coolcroo Castle

Clonamicklon Castle

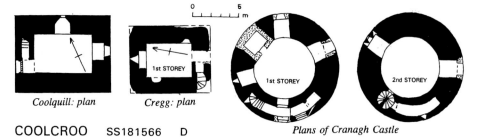

Coolquill: plan   Cregg: plan

Plans of Cranagh Castle

COOLCROO   SS181566   D

The northern half of a tower about 10.5m long by 9m wide stands 9m high, with evidence of one upper room over a vault reached by a narrow stair around the NE corner from a lost entrance facing east. The irregularly-shaped projection with a latrine in the angle between it and the main building is a later addition.

COOLQUILL   S251465   C

The cracked west wall of this tower measuring 10.5m by 8m contains a straight stair leading up from the entrance. The stair continues along the north side to reach a spiral stair in the NE corner which led to two upper levels above the third storey vault. One of the window-heads reset in an outbuilding came from these upper levels destroyed in the 1950s. The lowest level has a vault and the next two storeys have latrines in the SE corner. The adjoining farmhouse incorporates parts of a 17th century range. Coolquill was held by Morish Stoke in 1640 and later passed to Daniel Gahan.

CRAGG   R711654   D

This tower measuring 8.6m by 7.1m on a rock outcrop was held by John Mulryan in 1640. Much of the south wall containing chambers over an entrance passage is missing along with the staircase in the SW corner. The lowest level has an inserted fireplace in the west wall and remains of a cross-loop facing north. This level and the third storey were vaulted. The Civil Survey of 1654-6 also mentions a "barbican" or small bawn.

Coolquill Castle

Cramps Castle

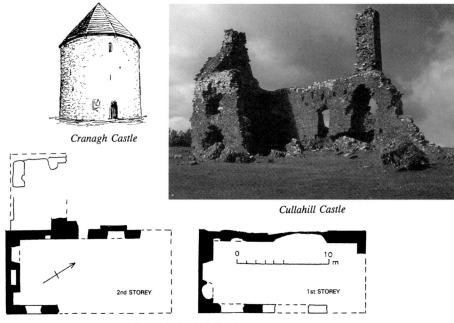

Cranagh Castle

Cullahill Castle

2nd STOREY

0   10
          m

1st STOREY

Plans of Cullahill Castle

CRAMPS   S218355   D

The earls of Ormond held this 18m high tower measuring 11.6m by 9.6m. Most of the west end wall containing chambers over the entrance has fallen but part of the stairwell remains visible, and the east and north walls have fine windows at fourth storey level.

CRANAGH   S162695   D

There is now a polygonal roof over the third storey of this truncated circular tower 11.8m in diameter over walling 2.8m thick. It was held by John Purcell in 1640 and was ruined by the 1650s. The second storey is dome-vaulted and has two window embrasures, one of which has two gunloops. The entrance lies on the SE side and leads to a pair of lobbies (both with murder holes in the ceilings), off which leads a spiral staircase. The third storey has a latrine on the west but was otherwise remodelled in the 18th century. A bawn of that period to the south encloses a group of buildings and incorporates older work, including the gable end of a 17th century house on the east side. An 18th century house adjoining the north side of the tower was mostly demolished a few years ago after a fire.

CULLAHILL   R989675   D

Set against a rock outcrop, upon which is the base of a wing or small tower, is a fragmentary 17th century house 18m long by 9m wide. Both storeys have fireplaces in the SW end wall (and an oven at the lower level), and the upper storey (with its former floor level with the top of the outcrop) has a fireplace with a projecting breast and high chimneystack on the NW side. Little remains of the house NE end. This building was held by Richard Burke in 1640. Nearby to the NE is a 30m diameter platform set above a drop to the river, probably a 13th century ringwork later occupied by the O'Dwyers.

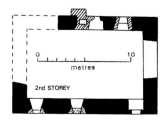

2nd STOREY

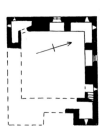

Drominagh: plan

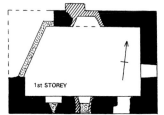

1st STOREY

Curraghcloney Castle

Plans of Dromineer Castle

Curraghcloney: plan

CURRAGHCLONEY   S166106   D

Only a fragment now remains of a Prendergast circular tower house about 11m in diameter over walls 2.5m thick. The basement has one complete embrasure with a loop flanked by gunloops, and traces of two others plus a latrine chute. Above was a dome-vaulted loft.

DERRY   R707776

A four storey tower measuring 7.5m by 6m over walls 1.5m thick lies on the west side of a fragmentary circular bawn 16m across with its 2m thick wall built upon a drystone cashel wall. The site is a crannog in Lough Derg. A thatched house mentioned in 1654-6 may be represented by the footings west of the tower. There is a staircase in the tower east wall, a damaged entrance in its north wall and a vault over its third storey.

DONOHILL   R906432

There are slight traces of a tower on a motte. It was already ruined by 1654, when it was held by the Countess of Ormond. In 1295 Sylvester le Archdeacon captured the castle and took bounty worth £500, although the malefactors within escaped via a postern gate.

DROMINAGH   R830983

The SE corner containing the spiral stairs of a tower measuring about 10m square 1.9m thick fell down in 1979. Now buried under rubble are an entrance in the south wall with a portcullis groove and a second entrance, ancient if not original, between the projections on the east side, where there was once a machicolation above. The basement, now full of rubble, was divided into two vaulted cellars. The second storey was also vaulted and has a damaged fireplace with a flue exiting halfway up the wall. A straight stair leads to the SW corner of the third storey, which has a two-light window facing west, a recess in the NW corner, and a stair leading up over a small room in the NE corner turret. Ranges extend north and south from the tower and to the west extends a bawn with remains of a gatehouse with a vaulted passageway on the north side. The castle lies beside Lough Derg and was taken in 1598 by Redmond Burke as a base for raiding the lands of the Earl of Clanrickard in Galway. It is described as "ruined" in the 1654 survey.

Dromineer Castle

Drumnamahane Castle

DROMINEER R814861 C

Very little remains of the three parallel vaults and two cross-walls later inserted into the lowest level of this hall-house beside Lough Derg, which measures 16.3m by 10.8m. and has lost its NW corner. Of the late 16th century or early 17th century are bawn walls enclosing the south and east sides, the ground level fireplace and its projecting breast on the north and the large windows on the south side serving a third storey created within former roof-space. Battlements still remain on the south side, and a higher SW turret. The original upper entrance remains at the east end of the south wall. The north wall has traces of arcading used to carry the wall-walk over the original roof, an arrangement similar to that found on 14th century buildings at St Davids and Swansea in South Wales. John Cantwell of Cantwell Court held the castle as a tenant of the Butlers in 1640. It may have been built by the Cantwells but was in O'Kennedy hands for much of 14th century.

Drumbane Castle

Drominagh Castle

DRUMBANE   S021561   D

In the 19th century this circular tower 9.2m in diameter stood five storeys high with vaults over the second and fourth storeys and there were twelve flat-headed loops, all of them damaged. Only the defaced lowest two levels containing rectangular rooms under a vault now remain, along with one jamb of the entrance, from which rises a staircase. See p133.

DRUMNAMAHANE   R948933

This tower measuring 12m by 11m has three pairs of double-splayed loops in each side of the lowest level except on the SE, where there were two projecting turrets, although the northern one has been destroyed. Straight stairs in this wall lead to the second storey, which was vaulted and had rooms in the turrets and two-light windows facing SE and NW, the embrasure of the latter having a murder hole covering the destroyed entrance lying in the recess between the turrets. From a third storey NE window embrasure there was access to a secret room in the haunch of the main vault. See page 133.

FARNEY   S067578   H

In 1640 James, Earl of Ormond held this circular tower house measuring 12.3m in diameter over walls 3.3m thick. The pointed-arched doorway on the south is blocked and entrance is now through the embrasure of a former loop facing west. Other loops facing east and north are unaltered. A stair rises from the entrance lobby to a spiral stair. Doorways from the stairs to mural chambers and to the three upper rooms over the dome-vaulted cellar are all blocked up, access now being though a 19th century extension on the SW side. These upper rooms all have 19th century windows facing east and north. At the summit corbels for machicolations survive on the east, north and west and there are chimney stacks on the SE and NE, but the parapet was rebuilt in the 19th century.

Farranrory Castle

Farney Castle

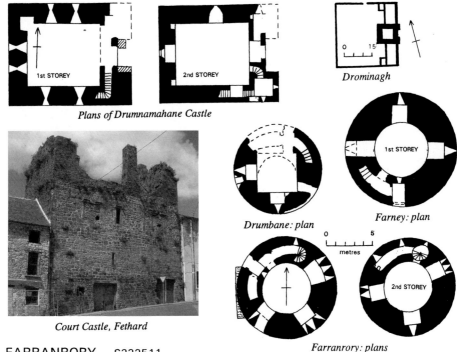

1st STOREY   2nd STOREY

Plans of Drumnamahane Castle

Drominagh

Court Castle, Fethard

Drumbane: plan

1st STOREY

Farney: plan

2nd STOREY

0   5
metres

Farranrory: plans

FARRANRORY   S332511

The Fannings held this castle as tenants of the Butlers. The badly cracked circular tower 10.4m in diameter over walling 2.6m thick was reduced in height to 7m in the early 20th century when most of the walling above the vault over the second storey was removed. Above the blocked pointed-arched entrance facing NW is a recess for a datestone or armorial panel. A passage leads to a spiral staircase on the north. Both the surviving levels have three embrasures with gunloops flanking a central vertical loop.

FETHARD   S207350   B

The town is still almost surrounded by the wall authorised by Edward III in 1376. A long section on the south side was restored in 1993, now having double-stepped merlons reaching 6m above the ground outside, although within the churchyard of Holy Trinity church just inside the wall the walkway within the parapet is only 2m above the ground. In the churchyard corner is a newly re-embattled three storey square tower with a higher west end, and there is a circular tower on the NE. A round arch still remains of the north gate, which had a D-shaped tower nearby to the east, but nothing survives of the east and west gates, the Wickett Gate facing NE or the Water Gate facing the bridge over the River Clashawley which protects the south and west sides. Beside the site of the Water Gate there is a sheela-na-gig upon the wall. East of the church is a ruined tower house about 13m long known as Court Castle with a shallow projection on the west side, north of which is a three-light 16th century window at third storey level. Both end walls were carried up one more level. South of it, upon the line of the town wall, is the partly restored Edmond's Castle, a rectangular tower with a two-light window and a latrine projection carried upon pyramidal corbels on the south side at third storey level. A later, more thinly walled and altered building north of the church retains a crucifixion panel.

Graigue Castle

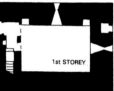

Grallagh: plans

Golden Castle

Bawn gunloops, Grallagh

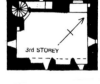

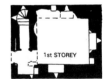

Gortmakellis: plans

Golden: plan

Gunloop at Golden

GALBERTSTOWN   S106531

At Galbertstown Lower there remains a section of a bawn wall 1.6m thick containing two low arches, possibly part of an internal arcade to carry a wall-walk. In the 19th century this remnant adjoined one of two gable ends of a 17th century house, now destroyed. Removal of rubble c1990 revealed the base of the south wall of a building to the north with a circular turret 3.2m in diameter on the SW corner. The other corners, now ruined or buried, are also said to have similar turrets.

GOLDEN   S011374   A

The northern half of a 16th century circular tower house lies beside the River Suir. The fragment contains a staircase and shows evidence of a cellar and a low loft under a vault, and one upper storey with one jamb each of a fireplace and a window embrasure. A gunloop facing NE has an oillet placed in the middle of a narrow slit.

GORTMAKELLIS S094435 C

The tower measures 10m by 7.8m and has four storeys with a pointed vault over the second. A third storey window has a pair of eliptical-headed lights. The roof contained an attic with gables flush with the outer end walls, although there were open wall-walks along the side walls and bartizans on the SW and NE corners. The entrance faces west. The castle was held by Matthew Pennefather in 1670.

GRAIGUE S124528

Of a bawn measuring 28m by 23m there remain a 5m high section of the 1m thick south wall with an external corbel west of a former gateway, a fragment of the west wall and footings of the east and north sides, against which lay an L-shaped house with two wings about 18m long by 8m wide. Little remains of the house apart from the 1.8m thick south end wall of the east wing, with a passage to a latrine in the SE corner.

GRALLAGH S155493 A

This tower measuring 12.4m by 9.8m has a vaulted cellar within the steeply battered base. Above are three upper storeys, the topmost of which has finely moulded two-light windows. Both ends rise up one more level, the NE end having another two-light window. A two-light window in the NW wall at second storey level is square-headed and must be a 16th century insertion. This level has a long passage leading to a latrine in the NE wall. The tower lay within a 16th century bawn of which there remains a 34m long and 2.5m high section of walling facing the road to the NE. It contains seven double-splayed gunloops taking the form of wide horizontal slits covered by huge slabs.

Gortmakellis Castle

Grallagh Castle

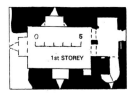

Plans of Graystown Castle

GRANTSTOWN   R969397   C

The fourth storey of this tower measuring 10m by 8.8m has a two-light window facing south and other windows with single ogival-headed lights on the other three sides, whilst the fifth storey has a mural room with a pair of ogival-headed windows in square-headed frames set either side of the SE corner. The lowest level has a double-splayed loop facing east and an entrance (with machicolation over) and staircase in the north wall.

GRAYSTOWN   S193459   C

Set upon a shelf of rock are remains of a 17th century bawn about 65m by 55m with a gateway on the north side. Only footings remain of the east wall, which lay on another, higher shelf. Just the north end remains of a house at the NW corner, with a damaged fireplace on the second storey and two small attic windows in the gable above. Above a cliff edge in the middle of the west side lies a 15th century tower house measuring 12.9m by 8.8m. It now lacks most of its south end, but the 20m high north wall contains rooms over the entrance and a broken spiral staircase with a NE angle-loop between the second and third levels. The fourth storey was vaulted and had a latrine in the west wall reached from the staircase by a long passage carried on an arch over the north end of the third storey room. There was also a chamber in the east wall at this level. Originally a seat of the Laffan family, Graystown passed in the 1650s to Gyles Cooke.

Graystown Castle   *Bawn wall at Graystown*

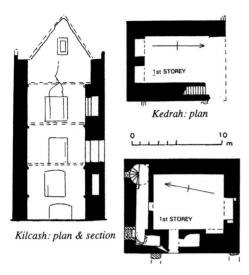

Kedrah: plan

Kilcash: plan & section

Ireton's Castle

IRETON'S   M867033

Over the round-arched entrance of this stronghouse measuring 10m square there was formerly a stone recording its construction c1650 by Sir Charles Coote. Lying in Lahinch townland, it was originally called Derry McEgan and the present name recalls one of Cromwell's generals, although he has no proven association with the castle. All three levels have fireplaces in the SE corner, where there is a chimney-stack and a square bartizan upon stepped corbels. At the SW and NE corners are pear-shaped flankers with gunloops. From the second storey upwards the flankers are circular, the pointed outer prows (which seem to be later additions) having at this level open platforms with parapets.

KEDRAH   S068280

A house adjoins the east side of a tower 10.8m by 8.6m which has lost its north wall. Part of a pointed vault remains over the second storey at the south end. A stair leads up in the east wall to a doorway in the SE corner of the third storey, which has a fireplace with a joggled lintel and a passage through the whole length of the south wall.

KILCASH   S326274   D

This late 16th or early 17th century Butler tower has high ivy-mantled walls of a later block to the west, and fragments of a bawn to the north. There are no vaults to any of the six storeys, the uppermost of which was an attic within the roof. There is a circular bartizan on the SE corner. The lowest storey shows signs of alterations, having a passage leading out to a spiral stair in the NE corner, but the entrance facing west towards the later wing must be old since it has a loop in the jamb and a machicolation high above it.

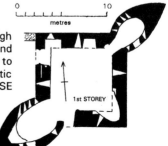

Plan of Ireton's Castle

Kilcooley Castle

Kilconnell Castle

KILCOLMAN   R819782

Projecting from the NW corner of the large courtyard of a lost 19th century house lies the west end of a three storey building 7.8m wide over walls 1m thick which was still roofed and complete in the early 19th century. The west wall has a blocked doorway. A "barbican and five thatcht tennements" are mentioned in the Civil Survey of 1654-6.

KILCONNELL   S141393

Of a tower once said to have measured 10.8m by 9.6m there remains only the precarious SW corner with evidence of a vault over the second storey and a stair linking two upper storeys, plus a circular bartizan set upon stepped corbels at the top. A bawn to the north has low and thin north and west walls containing gunloops.

KILCOOLEY or GRANGECASTLE   S307564   C

There are corbels for a machicolation over the entrance of this tower lying in the yard of a house. There are three upper storeys over a vaulted cellar and the west wall rises one stage higher. The east wall contains a spiral staircase and a latrine.

KILLAGHY   S330407   H

The five storey tower with an entrance in the west wall adjoining a 19th century house contains a hidden chamber reached by a trapdoor. The SW corner contains a spiral staircase. The third storey mullioned windows with square hoodmoulds must be 16th century insertions since two-light windows of the older later-medieval type survive in the east and west walls of the fifth storey, whilst the three lowest levels have large 19th century windows on the south side. Killaghy was held by the Tobins in 1650 but was then taken over and garrisoned with Commonwealth troops. It later went to the Greenes, then by marriage to the Despards, and later passed to the Wrights and other families.

Killaleigh Castle

Killahara Castle

KILLAHARA S094631 D

This tower measuring 12.2m by 9.6m set on a rock outcrop has mural chambers over an entrance passage in the NW wall, the spiral stair being in the north corner and a guardroom in the west corner. The second storey has a fireplace with joggled voussoirs and a latrine in the east corner. At the level of the third storey vault a passage leads from the stair to a second latrine in the east corner. The fourth storey was much altered in the 19th century, although it retains a secret room in the NE wall, and a keyhole-shaped gunloop facing SE. The lower levels have original windows of one or two lights with segmental or ogival heads. Stairs in the NW wall lead to the wall-walk.

KILLALEIGH R968940 D

This four storey O'Connor castle once bore the date 1601 over the round arched entrance protected by both external and internal machicolations. It is built on an unusual plan with a wing measuring 10m by 6.7m overlapping the west corner of a main block 15.5m long by 8.8m wide over walls 1.5m. A crossloop opens off the wide scale-and-platt staircase at the junction of the two parts and there is a gunloop higher up. There are circular bartizans on the north and south corners of the main block and on the west corner of the wing. The castle has five chimney stacks set upon gables rising off the outer walls but no original fireplaces remain. There are several hoodmoulded windows of one and two lights in the upper storeys, whilst the third storey of the main block has a pair of three-light windows facing SW. The brick vaults over the lowest level are 19th century insertions.

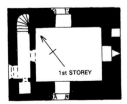

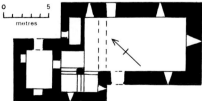

Plans of Killahara Castle

Plan of Killaleigh Castle

Killenure Castle

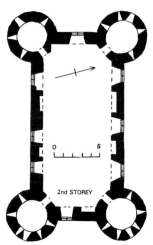

Killenure: plan

KILLENURE   S002438   D

The O'Dwyers' early 17th century stronghouse measuring 20.3m by 10.3m has been a ruin since at least 1793, when Austin Cooper made a sketch of it also depicting his own humble house nearby. It had been confiscated in the 1650s and given to the Clayton family. Above a low basement with small loops and the entrance doorway were two levels of living rooms with windows of two and three lights, plus an attic with small windows in the numerous gables surmounted by chimney stacks. Of the four corner towers 5.6m in diameter containing numerous gunloops the SE one adjoining a house remains roofed.

KILLOSKEHAN   S046700

A tower house of c1600 and a two storey high and six bay long early 18th century house west of it were both remodelled in 1865. The house replaced a 17th century wing mentioned in the Civil Survey of 1654-6, when it was held by Theobald Butler.

Killusty Castle

Keep at Kiltinan

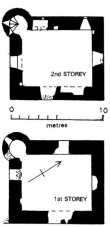

Killusty: plans

KILLOUGH   S510519

This still inhabited four storey tower has 18th century windows. The east end rises one storey higher and has an added bay. At the west end a wing shown on an 18th century map has been replaced by a more recent block.

KILLOWNEY or CASTLE WELLINGTON   R935817

Originally called Killowney, and held by Rory O'Kennedy in 1640, this ivy-covered tower measuring 12m by 9.2m was renamed after the Duke of Wellington built a house beside it in the 19th century. Originally there were three storeys below a vault and just one above but in the early 17th century an extra floor level was squeezed in at the top. At a level between that of the second and third storeys a passage off the staircase in the NW corner leads past four north-facing loops to a latrine in the NE corner. Higher up another passage in this wall leads to a chamber in the east haunch of the vault, whilst another chamber in the west haunch is reached directly off the staircase. The third storey has a fireplace in the south wall. The fourth storey has a mullion-and-transom window facing east and a window with two ogival-headed lights facing north. Stairs lead off the embrasure of the latter to a caphouse on the NW corner, off which was reached an open wall-walk on the north wall and a covered gallery, now ruined, on the west. A machicolation covers the entrance on the west side and there are bartizans on the NE and SW corners.

KILLUSTY   S250324   D

An inhabited 17th or 18th century block adjoins the SW end wall of a ruined three storey 16th or 17th century tower house measuring 10.4m by 8.8m wide over walls up to 1.4m thick. The tower has a circular stair turret on the west corner and corbels for a circular bartizan upon the east corner. The NW side has a fine fireplace at third storey level and the NE and SE sides have gables. The gable of another range lies at the far end of the inhabited part. The castle belonged to the O'Kearney family.

KILTINAN   R233320

The circular keep 10.3m in diameter upon a 30m high cliff above the west bank of the Clashawley River may be the work of Philip de Worcester, granted Kiltinan in 1215, or his successor. South of it lies a court and an inhabited mansion, which incorporates a rectangular medieval tower. The upper two storeys of the keep, reached by a spiral stair in a turret on the east side, were remodelled in the later medieval period, the second level having four loops and a doorway to a chamber upon the wall to the SW, whilst the third storey has a Sw window with two ogival-headed lights. The wall of the outer court to the west and NW also seems later medieval. It has a circular NE tower with gunloops and a square upper room. This seat of the Butler Lord Dunboyne was captured by Cromwell in 1649 after the bawn wall was breached by cannon. It was granted to Richard Stoper but sold in 1669 to Peter Cooke, whose descendants held the castle until 1921. The mansion was badly damaged by a fire started by intruders in 1979 but has been restored.

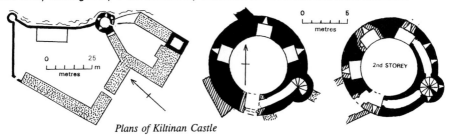

Plans of Kiltinan Castle

Knigh: plan

Knockane Castle

Knockagh Castle

1st STOREY   2nd STOREY   3rd STOREY   4th STOREY

0   5
metres

Plans & section of Knockagh Castle

KNIGH   R858847

A NW corner turret 4.6m square with two latrines in the vaulted second storey stands four storeys high but the main block measuring about 14m by 9m is reduced to footings. The ruin lies on a 2m high mound with a narrow ditch crossed by a causeway facing SW.

KNOCKAGH   S088697   C

In 1640 Sir John Morres held this circular tower house measuring 11.8m in diameter. The entrance on the NW has been destroyed. From it was reached a spiral stair on the NE. The lowest level is circular with one double-splayed loop, but the vaulted room above is squared off at the SE end. The third storey has a fine fireplace on the SW and a window with two segmental-headed lights facing SW, the embrasure having access to a chamber on the NW. The fourth storey has a similar layout but the lights of the NE window were ogival headed. The fifth storey also has a fireplace on the west, surmounted by a high chimney stack. There was an attic with the roof, of which the southern gable still remains. There are no remains of a late 17th century house to the south and a bawn with flankers mentioned in the early 19th century.

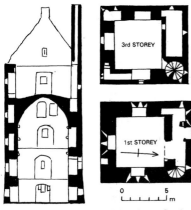

Plans and section of Knockane Castle

Knockgraffon Castle

Knockgraffon Motte

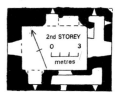

Knockgraffon: plan

KNOCKANE   R980792   C

There is a circular bartizan upon stepped corbels at the SW corner of this tower measuring 10m by 8.7m with gunloops flanking the basement loops which probably dates from c1600-20. The NE corner also once had a bartizan and contains a spiral staircase. There are small chambers over the entrance in the north wall, above which is a box-machicolation opening out of a gable with a dummy chimney. The south end wall also has a gable with another dummy chimney rising some 6m above the wall-walk, which is 15m above ground level. There were five main rooms, with a vault over the fourth level, plus an attic within the roof. The third storey has a fireplace on the west side, a latrine in the SE corner and a room in the SW corner with an angle-loop. The fifth storey also has a fireplace on the west, where there is a high chimneystack.

KNOCKGRAFFON   S045290 & 049295   C

Above the River Suir is a high motte with a summit 20m across having a bean-shaped bailey 40m by 70m to the NW. It was built in 1192 during an expedition against Donal Mor O'Brien, King of Thomond and given to William de Braose, but later regranted to Philip de Worcester. On the east side of the bailey is a fragment of a later stone building 5.6m wide. Not far away is a very ruined church with a large central tower and north transept which appear to have been adapted later as a stronghouse. In a field beyond it is a 16th century Butler tower measuring 11.5m by 8.7m with an east-facing entrance doorway. A long straight stair in the south wall rises to the foot of a spiral stair in the SW corner. There are circular bartizans on the NW and SE corners.

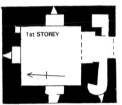

Bawn and flanker at Knockkelly

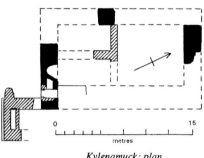

Kylenamuck: plan

Plans of Knockkelly Castle

KNOCKKELLY   S231079   D

The tiers of mullioned windows, the diagonally set chimneystacks and the gables flush with the outer walls betray the late 16th century date of this five storey tower measuring 12.3m by 10.2m with its south end wall rising one level higher. This end contains chambers over a hole where the entrance lay. At the third storey the spiral staircase in the SW corner has an angle-loop, the western chamber has another facing SW, and passages leading off the northern window embrasure to other angle-loops in the NW and NE corners, whilst there is a fireplace on the west side. The fourth storey has a fireplace on the south and a vault. The tower lies within an unusually complete bawn measuring 75m by 65m, the 5m high wall of which has a bartizan on the SW corner and circular flankers 5.8m in diameter with horizontal gunloops at the NW and SE corners. In the 18th century the Everard owners evicted the Keating tenants for non-payment of rent.

KYLENAMUCK   S027004   D

Lying within low and thin fragments of walling enclosing a bawn 50m across are very fragmentary remains of what seems to have been a hall-house 17.8m long by 10.7m wide. The south end wall contains a stair leading up from an upper floor doorway and has abutting against it two vaults supported upon inserted crosswalls. Little remains of what appears to have been a southerly extension 4m wide, but a latrine turret projecting east from the extension still partly stands three storeys high.

LACKEEN   M951042   A

A stair in the NE wall of this tower measuring 11.8m by 10.4m leads up from the south-facing entrance to the foot of a spiral stair in the west corner. The second storey has a fireplace in the SE wall and a mural chamber in the NE wall. The third storey is an unlit vaulted loft with a chamber in its NE wall reached off the spiral stair. The top storey has arcading at the NE end, where there is a window with tracery. A stair with a north angle-loop leads to a gallery with an east angle-loop in the thickened wall over the arcading. The corbels remain of a machicolation over the entrance and round bartizans on the north and south corners. The stepped gables must be a later modification. An attic room seems to have had dormer windows along the sides of the roof. The tower lies in a pentagonal bawn about 56m by 45m with a round-arched gateway near the NE corner. The castle belonged to Brian O'Kennedy, who died in 1588. It was confiscated by Cromwell in 1653.

LATTERAGH   R976726   C

A fragment 2.6m thick of a circular keep lies upon a platform 23m square with a 3m high retaining wall 1.1m thick. The castle probably existed by 1254, when William de Marisco was allowed a weekly market here and is first mentioned in 1269. It was held by John Laffan in 1384 and by Sir John Morris in 1640, but was ruined by the 1650s. See p148

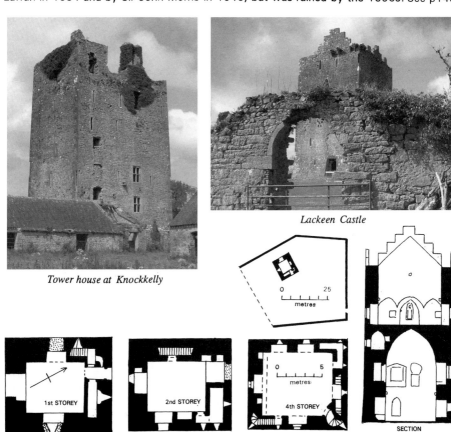

Tower house at Knockkelly

Lackeen Castle

Plans & section of Lackeen Castle

Lisbunny Castle

Liskeveen Castle

LISBUNNY   R892794   C

Beside a stream is a hall house 16.9m long by 11.4m wide over walls 1.8m thick above a battered plinth. It is probably 13th century, although the fireplace of the upper storey and the width of the openings at that level suggest a 16th or 17th century remodelling, when a third storey was created above. Beside the entrance in the east wall at second storey level is part of the well of a spiral stair which probably had wooden steps.

LISKEVEEN   S171524

The thinly-walled upper parts of this tower measuring 10m by 9.6m date from the 19th century. No vaults or old fireplaces have survived the gutting of the interior, but original features include the western side of the entrance on the south side with a staircase rising from it, a latrine chute on the north side. and the second storey angle-loops with flanking gunloops in the NW and SW corners. Against the east wall is a gable-mark of a later range. In the 1650s the castle was held by Thomas Butler of Kilconell, an "Irish Papist".

Latteragh Castle

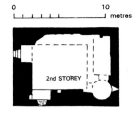

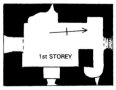

Lismallin: plans

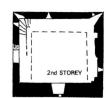

Liskeveene: plans

Lismallin Castle

Loughlohery Castle

LISMALLIN   S313442

This building measuring 11.8m by 8.7m had small rooms over a blocked entrance facing north towards a farmyard. There was a spiral staircase in the NE corner. The interior, now very defaced, has remains of three unvaulted storeys with blocked-up windows.

LOUGHLOHERY   S086238   C

This late 16th century tower belonging to the Keating family measures 11.4m by 9.5m and has four storeys with the second storey vaulted. There was also an attic in the roof, which had gables on all four sides, and there are circular bartizans set on two diagonally opposite corners. The hall on the third storey has a fireplace and four angle loops each with gunloops on either side. There is a drain for emptying chamber pots beside one of these angle-loops. The fourth storey contained a private suite of two rooms. A second castle called Coolbane once lay at S086236 in the field on the opposite side of the road.

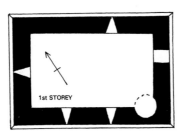

Loughlohery: plan   *Plans of Lisbunny Castle*

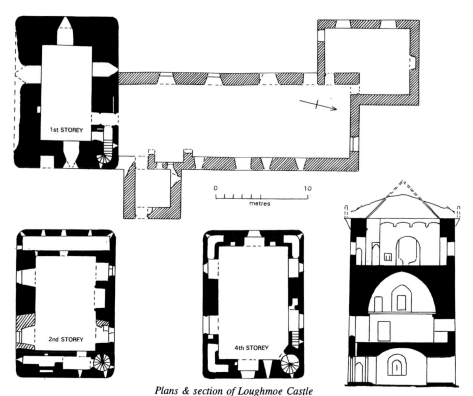

Plans & section of Loughmoe Castle

LOUGHMOE   S115672   G

The round-cornered 15th century tower 16m long by 11.8m wide and 17m high to the wall-walk is a fine specimen despite the loss of the parapet with machicolations in the middle of each side and the defacement of the south side. A spiral stair in the NE corner connects four storeys with a segmental vault over the first and a pointed vault over the third. The ends are carried up to contain fifth storey rooms at wall-walk level, the east end being thickened above the top room by an arcade. The second storey forming the main private room has a fine 17th century fireplace with the initials of one of the Purcells, the last of whom, Colonel Nicholas, a Jacobite signatory of the Treaty of Limerick in 1691, died in 1722. There are rooms in the end walls, that at second storey level at the west end being the full width of the tower and having angle loops, whilst there is a latrine at the east end. The fourth storey has three corner rooms, those at the west end having angle-loops, whilst that in the SE corner is set some way above the main room floor.

In the early 17th century a 26m long mansion of four storeys with large upper mullion-and-transom windows and stringcourses marking the floor levels was added to the north side, which contains the entrance with drawbar slots and a stair to the foot of a spiral stair in the NE corner. Beside this corner the mansion has a porch which faced the former bawn to the east and which has holes in the outer doorway jamb and arch, plus many gunloops. A large ground level fireplace backs onto the porch. Clasping the NW corner of the mansion is a large wing containing five storeys of private rooms formerly linked by a wooden staircase. The wall-walks on the mansion have parapets with the middle part of each merlon made into a semi-circle surmounted by a finial.

Loughmoe Castle

Mellison: plan

Loughmoe Castle

MELLISON   S263532   C

The cellar of this tower measuring 7m by 5.5m has recesses on the north and south sides and a double-splayed loop facing west. Above the second storey vault are two upper levels with latrines in the NE corner. At this level the east wall is corbelled out between the projection containing the chutes and the remains of a tiny circular SE stair turret,

Fireplace at Loughmoe

Mellison Castle

Moorstown Castle

Milltown St John Castle

MILLTOWN ST JOHN   S230402

The arms of the St Johns and Hacket families appear upon this 16th century five storey tower measuring 10.2m by 8.4m beside an inhabited house. The lowest level has loops flanked by gunloops and a crossloop facing towards the lobby of the entrance in the west wall. The third storey lying over a vault has access to a western room with a gunloop and a SW angle-loop. There is also a latrine with a NE angle-loop and a small room in the SE corner, each of them reached off the embrasures of windows of two lights with elliptical-shaped heads flanked by gunloops. The south side has an altered fireplace and the next two levels have fireplaces on the north side. Above both sides chimney stacks rise to 19m above ground, and a gable with a sixth storey attic window survives at the east end, whilst there is a gabled caphouse over the spiral staircase in the NW corner.

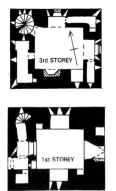

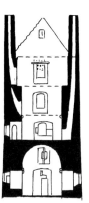

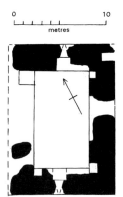

Milltown St John: plans & section

Modeshill: plan

Mortlestown: plans

MODESHILL   S352433   D

Just to the NW of a medieval church ruin lie the defaced and overgrown remains of the lowest part of one of Tipperary's largest tower houses, a building 16m long by 11.6m wide over 2.8m thick walls up to 4.5m high. There is a latrine chute at the eastern corner.

MOORSTOWN   S116262

Perched on a rock is a circular tower 10.4m in diameter over walling 2.8m thick. Below a vault are two circular rooms each with their loops flanked by gunloops and above are two further inaccessible storeys of square rooms with latrines on the west side. At the summit are gables rising from the outer edge of the walling on the SW and NE, the latter having a chimneystack upon it. The parapet is corbelled out and has a machicolation facing west. The entrance facing SE is flanked by a guard room and a passage leading to a destroyed spiral staircase. The tower lies just inside the west wall of a bawn measuring 55m by 42m with circular NE and SW corner flankers. South of the tower extends a range of later two storey buildings and on the east side is an internally projecting gatehouse about 7.8m square with the outer entrance deeply recessed to allow a murder hole to cover the outside of the gate. Further south a modern gap has been made in the bawn east wall. In the 1650s Moorstown was taken from the Keatings and given to the Greens.

MORTLESTOWN   S219431   D

Named after the Martels, granted this estate in the 1650s, this building measuring 9.6m by 8.2m has an entrance set in a slight projection from the east wall, an arrangement making nonsense of the former machicolation above. From the entrance a straight stair rises in the south wall to where a SW corner spiral stair begins at third storey level. This room lies over a vault and has a fireplace and a hatch into a chamber in the vault haunch. Two deep embrasures, one with access to a latrine, have recently been repaired. Above was a low fourth storey, and there was an additional fifth level at the west end.

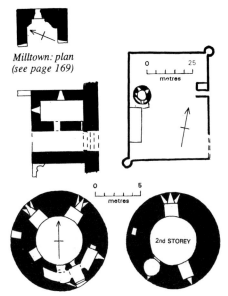

*Milltown: plan
(see page 169)*

Plans of Moorstown Castle

Mortlestown Castle

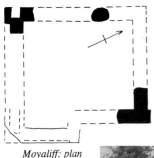

Moyaliff: plan

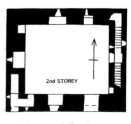

Plan & section of Moyneard Castle

Moyaliff Castle

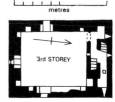

Moycarkey: plan

MOYALIFF   S043556

On the 8m high summit of a mound near a house are very fragmentary remains of an early keep measuring about 15.5m by 12m. The 3m high SE wall has its southern part projecting out beyond the rest. The west corner has a latrine chute. This keep may be the tower which is mentioned in 1338 as covered in shingles but valueless because no-one wanted to rent it from the owner, James Butler, Earl of Ormond.

MOYCARKEY   S145528   D

This tower measuring 11.3m by 8.1m is unusual in that the thick east end wall containing the entrance only contains rooms from the fourth storey level upwards. Below are straight stairs and latrines, and two deep recesses at ground level. The third storey lying over a vault has a fireplace on the east side. A secret chamber is reached by a hatch in the floor of the access passage to the main fourth storey room. The fifth storey has a west window of two ogival-headed lights with a hoodmould. The ends of the former joists of the floor of this level are visible in the outer wall-face below this window. The attic in the roof is thought to have had a fireplace. The north end wall has two more levels, the wall-walk passing through it as a passage with a vaulted chamber above, There is a circular bartizan on the SW corner and a box-machicolation covers the entrance. A sheela-na-gig has been removed from the south wall. The tower lies within a bawn measuring 53m by 44m with a fragmentary wall 1.5m thick with three storey circular flankers 5.8m in diameter at the NE and SW corners and a bartizan on the NW corner. The flankers have staircases following the wall curvature and numerous gunloops but the NE one was remodelled as a gazebo with large new windows in the early 19th century. The SW flanker has corbels for a bartizan on the south side. The castle was held by William Cantwell in 1640.

MOYNEARD   R189635   C

This tower measuring 13.8m by 11.6m over walls 2m thick has straight flights of stairs rising in the east wall from a blocked entrance facing north. The first and third storeys have vaults, nothing now surviving above the latter. A latrine chute in the SW corner was adapted as a flue for a fireplace inserted in the basement in the 18th century. There are buried footings of a bawn and an outbuilding to the west and north.

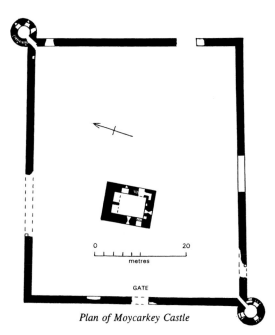

Plan of Moycarkey Castle

Moycarkey Castle

MULLINAHONE   S336400   C

In the yard beside one of the roads in the village stand the north, south and east walls of a large building now mostly obscured by ivy. On the south side is what looks like an upper floor doorway. This and the lack of any large windows between this level and the fragmentary parapet suggests that the building may be a 13th century hall-house.

Bawn flanker at Moycarkey

Mullinahone Castle

Nicholastown Castle

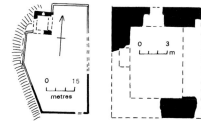

Hall block at Nenagh

NENAGH   R867791   A

Nicholastown: plans

Theobald Walter's castle of c1200-20 lay at the north corner of a triangular walled town and comprised a circular keep 16m in diameter with walls up to 4.6m thick standing at one corner of a pentagonal court 37m across with circular towers up to 10m in diameter at the other corners. The curtain wall and west tower have been destroyed and only a fragment remains of the east tower. One of the two southern towers, between which was the gateway, remains fairly complete, along with the rectangular back of the gatehouse, probably of c1300, which contained a hall over the inner part of the passage. The outer part of the passage retains a portcullis groove and a drawbridge pit has been traced by excavation. The well-preserved keep was heightened to 30m by the addition c1860 of a folly top storey. Originally it rose about 22m to the wall-walk and was entered at the second of four storeys. Only a trapdoor gave access to the unlit basement room now reached from outside by a modern passage. A spiral stair then rises to the hall and chamber on the third and fourth storeys, both of which have fireplaces. From the hall a dog-leg shaped passage leads out of a window embrasure to the former wall-walk of the NW curtain. A similar passage above leads to a latrine in a corbelled-out projection. Theobald Walter's descendants the Butlers abandoned Nenagh to the O'Briens in the late 14th century, but it was recovered in 1533 by Sir Piers Butler, who later became Earl of Ormond. The castle was burnt by the O'Carrolls in 1548. It was captured by Eoghan Rua O'Neill in 1646 but was recaptured by Murrough O'Brien, only to be surrendered in 1650 to General Ireton after a short siege. The O'Carrolls seized Nenagh in 1689 but General Ginckell captured the castle for William III after a siege lasting just one day, and the defences were then slighted. Nothing remains of the town defences.

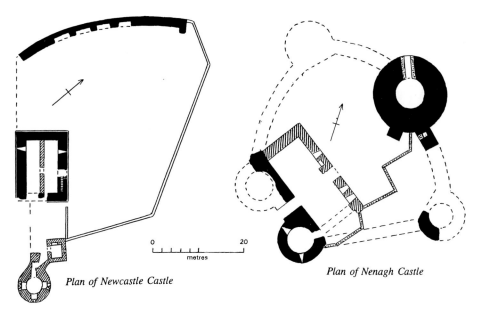

Plan of Newcastle Castle

Plan of Nenagh Castle

NEWCASTLE   S126136   D

On level ground beside the River Suir is an enclosure about 40m across with only a low and thin wall probably of recent date towards the river but with the curved west side enclosed by a 13th or 14th century wall 2m thick and 3.5m high in the inner side of which are a number of pointed arches 2.8m wide, 0.9m deep and 1.8m high. On the SW is a building 14.6m long by 11m wide over walls 2m thick, also likely to be 13th century. The narrow and crudely built stair rising around the east corner must be original but later insertions are the doorway covered by a loop opening off the stair and the lengthways crosswall and pair of vaults over the lowest level. The upper parts are very ruinous and obscured by ivy. About 14m beyond the 19th century opening in the SW end wall is a 16th century round tower 7m in diameter covered in ivy but complete to the parapet. There are two habitable upper rooms connected by a stair set over a basement with its own separate entrance and loops flanked by gunloops. A latrine at second storey level overhangs the outer face of a wall connecting the tower to a small rectangular building to the North. Newcastle was the main seat of the Prendergast family.

NICHOLASTOWN   S118226   D

There is a cliff below the western side of a bawn 60m long by 35m wide belonging to the Keating family. Most of the southern half of the 0.7m thick wall stands complete to a coped top (without a wall-walk or parapet) 3.5m above ground and footings are visible of the rest. Nothing remains of the house mentioned in the 17th century but of a tower house measuring 12m by 10.2m in the NW corner the north wall still partly stands four storeys high with a bartizan on the NW corner and there is a lower fragment of the SE corner.

NODSTOWN   S067048   D

Lying amongst farm buildings is a tower with the east side having a blocked entrance and a latrine-chute at ground level and a two-light window at fourth storey level. The north end wall is continued up one storey higher, with another two-light window.

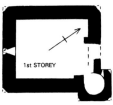

Rathnaveoge: plans

PORTLAND   R890071

Only the lowest storey now full of rubble remains of a tower measuring 10.4m by 7.2m. Eoghan O'Madden is said to have built this castle in the 14th century. It was captured by William MacUachtrach Burke in 1441 and by Redmond Burke in 1600.

POULAKERRY   S298234   D

The parapet of this still-inhabited tower with a north-facing pointed-headed entrance has lost its double-stepped merlons. The NE corner contains a spiral staircase and the NW corner has an angle-loop at the level of the fourth storey, which is vaulted. The fifth storey windows are larger than the others but are still only of one wide light.

POWERSTOWN   S226248   D

There are two vaulted rooms each with their own separate entrances in the lowest level of this building measuring 8.4m by 6.9m. At least one upper level survives but is obscured by vegetation and no longer accessible since no stairs remain.

RAHELTY   S170613

In 1640 Theobald Purcell of Loughmoe held this round-cornered tower measuring 13.2m by 10m. It contains a vaulted cellar and three upper storeys, the lowest of which has a passage in the south wall leading to a latrine in the SW corner from a spiral staircase in the SE. One of the centrally-placed former machicolations protected the entrance on the east side. The fourth storey has windows with two ogival-headed lights.

Redwood Castle

Poulakerry Castle   *Rahelty Castle*

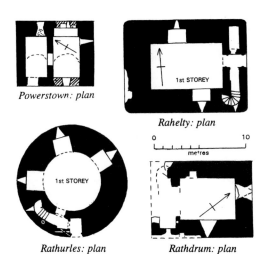

Powerstown: plan

Rahelty: plan

Rathurles: plan   *Rathdrum: plan*

Doorway at Rathurles

RATHDRUM   S182326

Of a tower measuring 11m by 8.1m there remain only the cellar, with two loops, and parts of the storey above, which was vaulted. Little remains of the south end wall containing chambers over an entrance flanked by a guardroom on the SE and a stair on the SW. One of the lost upper storeys had a latrine on the east side, where its chute remains.

RATHNAVEOGE   S081839   D

This tower measuring 10.8m by 9.1m on an outcrop was held by John Magher in 1654, when it was described as unfinished, probably having been begun c1640. Three upper levels with wooden-lintelled window embrasures were reached by a spiral stair in a square turret clasping the east corner. Below the destroyed entrance on the NE was commanded by gunloops and is surmounted by a gabled niche for a plaque bearing heraldic arms or a date and initials. The second and third storeys have fireplaces in the SW wall and the fourth storey has a fine fireplace in the NE wall.

RATHURLES   R907800

Hidden away in shrubs near the Ollatrim River is the stump of a 16th century circular tower 12m in diameter over walls 2.9m thick now broken down above the level of the dome vault over the second storey. An upper level had a latrine on the SW side.
The passage from the pointed-headed entrance leads only to the spiral staircase and a double turn has to be made to reach the cellar, which has three loops. The castle belonged to the O'Kennedy Donn family of Upper Ormond. A nearby church lies with a ringfort.

REDWOOD   M929098   D

This tower measuring 16.5m by 13.2m over walls 2.8m thick has an entrance in a recess between two turrets in the middle of the east side, where there is a sheela-na-gig under a modern balcony. The SE turret contains latrines at two upper levels, where the windows are all modern insertions. Most of the parapet with a bartizan on the SW corner and a chimney stack on the north side also represent modern rebuilding. Probably 15th century, but remodelled c1600, the castle is said to have been a school of history and law run by the MacEgans during the 16th and 17th centuries.

Roosca Castle

Gatehouse at Roscrea

ROCHESTOWN   S071199

This tower amongst farm buildings measures 12.2m by 9m with the south and east walls 1.7m thick. The blocked entrance lies at the south end of the west wall which is 2.6m thick and contains a stair rising to the foot of a spiral stair in the NW corner at the third storey level, which is much overgrown with ivy and the parts above destroyed. The second storey has a nearly square southern room with a SW corner mural chamber over the entrance. A latrine passage in the NE corner has been adapted to give access to a smaller northern room, now filled by a large tank. In 1641 the Butlers besieged Thomas Grove here for five weeks until the wall of the vanished bawn was breached. A siege engine brought against the tower was broken by stones thrown from it. In 1647 the castle was stormed and burned by Lord Inchiquin and its defenders killed.

ROOSCA   S051196   D

A 16th century house measuring 19m by 10m over walls 1m thick and containing two ogival-headed loops facing west on the uppermost of two storeys is built on a rocky shelf so that the ground drops away dramatically to the south and west but rises to the upper floor level on the north. A slop drain on the west side probably marks the position of a kitchen. The featureless gable walls stand complete but the north end of the west wall and the south end of the east wall have fallen. A thin wall still standing 5m high in a fragment at the NW corner enclosed an irregularly shaped bawn extending 21m to the north of the house and 20m to the east of it. On the NW is an added D-shaped flanker 4.8m in diameter over walls 0.6m thick with several gunloops on two levels. This Burke castle was captured in the 1640s by Lord Inchiquin and the garrison all killed.

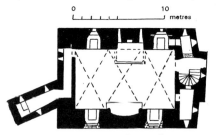

Roscrea: gatehouse plan

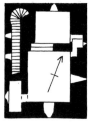

Rochestown: plan

Rochestown Castle

ROSCREA S137894 E

King John's earth and timber castle of 1214 was replaced by
a loopholed stone curtain wall around a D-shaped bailey up to
60m across in the 1280s, after Edward I recovered Roscrea
from the Bishop of Killaloe. There is a circular tower 8m in
diameter with two levels of crossloops at the SW corner with
an adjoining postern commanded by a machicolation, and
there is a U-shaped tower 10m wide on the SE side. The
curtain is intact except for a 23m wide gap on the south
where a later wing of the early 18th century Damer House
extends towards it. On the north side is a rectangular tower
measuring 16.3m by 10.3m which had a gateway passage
flanked by guard rooms, with a subterranean prison below the
western one. The walls dividing off the guard rooms are not
original. The upper levels were altered when the building was
later converted into a tower house, and have also had some
some modern restoration, but the hall over the entrance
passage has an original rib-vault of three bays and a fine
fireplace. There is a spiral stair on the east side, a long
passage out to a latrine in the curtain wall on the west side,
and windows facing north and south, the former with seats in
the embrasures. The end walls contain further chambers and
stairs higher up. From 1315 until 1689 Roscrea was held by
the Butler earls of Ormonde, whose arms appear in stucco
work on an upper storey fireplace in the SW tower. The castle
was used as a military post during the 19th century.

Roscrea Castle

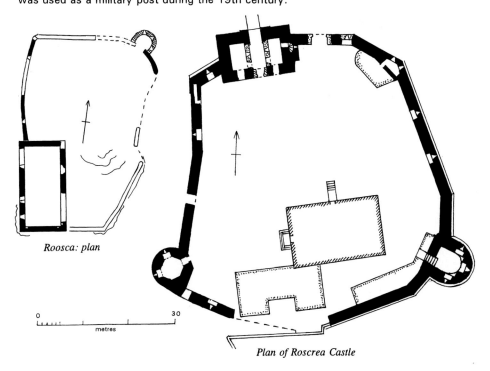

Roosca: plan

0   30
metres

Plan of Roscrea Castle

SHANBALLYDUFF   SO55372

There are circular three storey high flankers at the SW and NE corners of the bawn and a tower house on a rock platform in the middle still stands 12m high with evidence of four storeys connected by a staircase in the SE corner. There are chambers over the entrance on the east side, whilst the south side has a blocked three-light window at third storey level and a two-light window at fourth storey level, both of them 16th century type openings with hoodmoulds. Another indication of the tower's comparatively late date is the recess over the pointed-arched entrance for a former datestone or armorial panel.

SHORTCASTLE   S084278

To the west of the farmhouse lies a tower now reduced down to its second storey, which has ogival-headed loops facing east and north. NW of the tower is a hole in the ground.

SLAINSTOWN   S220385

The SW corner of this tower measuring 7.7m by 7m is broken down above the level of the vault over the second storey. A stair in the south wall leads up from a defaced entrance facing towards where a later two storey range 8m wide extends 15.2m to the east. Little remains of the north and east walls of this range.

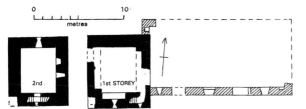

Plans of Slainstown Castle

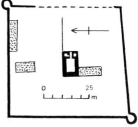

Shanballyduff: plan

Shanballyduff Castle

Slainstown Castle

Suir Castle

Synone Castle

SUIR   R004352

There are two secret rooms set one above the other on the east side of this Butler tower measuring 12.2m by 9.8m. The west wall lying close to a cliff-edge contains a straight stair leading from the entrance up to where a spiral stair began at the third storey. This level has a vaulted main room and an L-shaped room in the SE corner, whilst a passage runs the length of the west wall to a latrine with its chute opening out of the north wall at second storey level. The second storey floor was carried upon beams carried within holes in the walls, without any corbels, wall-plate or offset. The fourth storey is no longer accessible. The north end wall rises one level higher and there are remains of circular SW and NE corner bartizans. In 1636 Sir John Bourke sold the castle to John Cantwell.

SYNONE   S089463   C

There are three machicolations on the summit of this circular tower house 9m in diameter over walls 2.2m thick. The tower is 15m high and has vaults over the first and third of the four storeys. Adjoining it is the corner of a two storey building.

```
0                    10
|__|__|__|__|__|__|__|
        metres
```

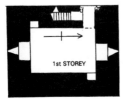

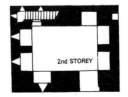

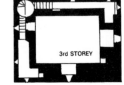

Plans of Suir Castle

TEMPLEMORE   S108718   A

Templemore Lake protected the north and east sides of a bawn measuring about 50m by 40m. Fragments of the 1.5m thick curtain wall adjoin an early keep 16.5m by 11m over walls 2.6m thick above an added battered base lying on higher ground at the SW corner. The parts of the north and east walls within the bawn have been destroyed. The south and west walls have pilaster buttresses, suggesting a date of c1200, and there is a latrine-chute in the NW corner. The third storey with a gallery in the west wall and the attic within the roof were also probably the result of later medieval modifications, whilst the circular turret and bellcote on top of the walls and the vault in the NW corner of the lowest storey appear to be 19th century.

TERRYGLASS   R859010 and 863004   A

Terryglass was a Butler possession from the 13th century until at least the 1640s. In the village are three sides of a late 16th century bawn about 28m square on the site of a former college with the wall-walk and parapet remaining on a wall 1.2m thick. Only one corner with a circular bartizan remains of a stronghouse with formed the fourth side. There is a round arched entrance on the east with drawbar slots and hanging eyes.

Not far away lies a 13th century keep known as Old Court, of great interest despite being ruined above the base of the second storey. Above plinths rising as much as 4m high it measures 20.5m by 16.3m over walls up to 2.8m thick. The basement has a loop in each wall and has a later cross-wall, although there are no signs of vaults and the next floor was carried on an offset in the sidewalls. There are four round towers at the corners, the southern ones being 9m in diameter, whilst the NE tower has rooms similar in size but within thinner outer walls. Here the lowest level was a prison reached only by a trapdoor from above. The small NW tower contains a spiral staircase reached by a round-headed doorway, beside which is the entrance. There is the base of a second stair leading up from the second storey in the west wall. A stub of a bawn wall adjoins the SE tower.

Templemore Castle

Old Court, Terryglass

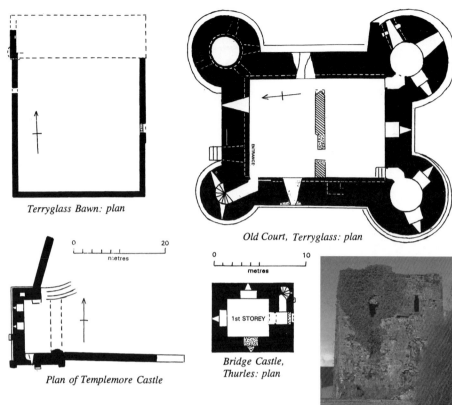

Terryglass Bawn: plan

Old Court, Terryglass: plan

0   20
n:etres

0   10
metres

Bridge Castle,
Thurles: plan

Plan of Templemore Castle

Tower at Thurles

THURLES   S128586 & 128587   C

Nothing remains of the town walls and a motte at the west end of the town was destroyed c1800. Upon it stood a manorial complex once known as Durlas Castle but later replaced by a 16th century bawn with flankers known as Croak Castle. A tower called Black Castle behind a house in Liberty Square in the NW corner of the walled town superseded it as the Butler seat in the town. Used more recently as an abattoir, this building has four storeys with the first and third vaulted. The blocked original entrance in the east wall led into a lobby with a covering cruciform loop. A mural chamber above has a latrine in the SE corner. The third storey has single light ogival-headed windows and the fourth storey has two light ogival-headed windows. Fragments of the parapet remain along with corbels for a bartizan on the SW corner. There seems to have been a 17th century range on the west side, and to the north are fragments of a bawn, one with a bartizan, although much of it was demolished in the late 20th century.

At the east end of Liberty Square is a second tower called Bridge Castle, said to have been built in 1453 and measuring 8.8m by 7.3m. It adjoined the east gate of the town, one jamb of which adjoins the north wall, where there is blocked doorway. However the main entrance seems to have been in the west wall beside the spiral stair in the NW corner. The basement now serves as a shop. The second storey is vaulted and has a latrine in the north wall, which another latrine leads off the staircase higher up. The third storey has windows of single and paired ogival-headed lights and an arcade to carry the south gable of the modern roof containing an attic room. The stepped parapet is mostly original apart from some rebuilding on the west side in the late 20th century.

Tombrickane Castle

Thurlesbeg Castle

THURLESBEG   R075440

Only the bases remain of circular turrets 2.2m and 3m in diameter respectively on the NE and NW corners of a building 16.7m long by 11m wide. The dimensions suggest a 13th century hall-house but the surviving features in the 9m high eastern half of the south wall suggest a 15th or 16th century date, with a double-splayed basement loop and a passage higher up. A jamb of a doorway of that period lies loose in the field nearby to the west. This MacGrath seat passed to the Fulwars in the 1650s.

TOMBRICKANE   R886957   C

This tower measuring 13.3m by 9.8m over walls 2.1m thick has lost most of its SW corner which contained a latrine at second storey level, and another beside the third storey vault. There is vault over the topmost of a tier of rooms over the destroyed entrance in the east wall and there is a spiral stair in the SE corner. The third storey has a fireplace in the north wall and the subsidiary eastern room leading off it has a broken NE angle-loop. On the NW corner are corbels for a former bartizan. In the 1650s the castle belonged to Rory and William Kennedy.

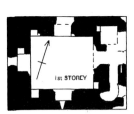

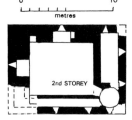

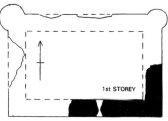

Plans of Tombrickane Castle   *Plan of Thurlesbeg Castle*

TULLAUN   R846915   D

Hanging eyes remain inside the doorways from the stair to the upper rooms of this 16m high tower measuring 11.2m by 8.8m on a rock outcrop. At second storey level the spiral stair in the SE corner has an angle-loop, and off it leads a passage to a latrine in the SW corner. The third storey is vaulted, has a subsidiary room with a NE angle-loop. The main room has windows with ogival-headed lights, in pairs on the north and the south, the latter having a transom. The west window embrasure has access down into a secret chamber in the NW corner.

TULLOW   S191718

Possibly built by the O'Mahers in the 14th century, but held by Piers Butler in 1640, this building is unusual in having a circular tower 6.2m projecting from the north corner which has a spiral stair serving the upper storeys carried on a round squint-arch above the angle between the tower and the main block. The round tower fourth storey has a dome-vault but none of the three main levels of the main block was vaulted. There are remains of crossloops with bottom roundels in the corner tower. They were later partly obscured by a change in the floor levels associated with the insertion of fireplaces in the second and third storey rooms. The main block end wall adjoining the tower contains fireplaces, that on the top level (now fallen) being a 17th century insertion. From the second storey a doorway leads out onto the where there was a wall-walk on a bawn wall 1.4m thick and 3.6m high.

Tullaun Castle

Tullow Castle

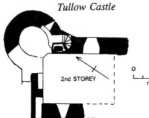

Plans of Tullow Castle

*Tullaun:
plans & section*

OTHER CASTLE REMAINS IN COUNTY TIPPERARY

ASHLEYPARK R879859 4m high fragment of NE corner with traces of vault set on 18m diameter island (a crannog?) drowned by raising of water level of Lough Ourna.

BALLYARTELLA R839834 Fragment of east wall and base of north wall of tower beside Nenagh River held by Countess of Ormond in 1650s.

BALLYCAHILL S843766 Fallen fragments of tower upon summit of possible motte.

BALLYDAVID S180543 Fragment of tower north wall with ogival-headed loop in outbuilding of 19th century house. Held by James, Earl of Ormond in 1640.

BALLYHAUGH M940002 Collapsed in 1839. Rubble covered base of tower with entrance, guardroom and stair in south wall. Ogival-headed loop in nearby shed.

BALLYMACADAM S077234 Low ivy-covered ruin about 7m wide.

BALLYNAHINCH S023411 One low thin featureless fragment and footings only.

BALLYNAMONA S001413 Fragment remains in outbuildings south of house. Granted to the Westons in the 1650s.

BALLYNAVIN R946912 Fragment of bawn wall with gunloop adjoins 19th century house. Described in 1654-6 survey as a "new castle not finished the walls only standing.

BALLYNEILL S367257 Corner flanker 4.2m in diameter and flagment of north wall is all that remains of an O'Neill seat granted in 1650s to John Spillman.

BANSHA R955332 Roadside shrine built into stump of tower about 11.5m long NW-SE with walls up to 2.5m thick. Buried passage on SE and part of stairwell on SW.

BAPTIST GRANGE S211301 Low defaced fragments 1.4m thick to south of medieval church. Nearby motte destroyed c1850.

BLEAN R994779 30m long house lacking cut stone. May incorporate part of castle held by Marcus Magrath in 1640. Thick fallen fragment nearby. Evidence of bawn to north.

BROWNSTOWN S137647 9m long, 2m thick south end wall of tower held in 1640 by Theobald Purcell. Traces of SE corner spiral staircase and one destroyed loop.

CARRIGATOGHER R819766 Footings of D-shaped bawn flanker and building north of it.

CASTLEBLAKE S134330 Four storey tower within pig-farm complex. No access allowed.

CASTLELEAKE S039406 Named after 18th century clergyman Matthew Leake. Later used as distillery and then as a workhouse, and consequently much altered.

CASTLELOUGH R737829 SE corner four storeys high, remains of east wall 15m long and fallen fragments on island in Lough Derg. Remains of staircase and basement vault.

CASTLEPARK S008384 Part of vault of Butler tower 8.8m wide with straight stair in north wall up to two upper storeys of which only east wall remains.

CLOGABREEDY S062278 High fragment of north wall of this Burke tower shows two upper storeys over a vault. Footings of a later range or bawn adjoin a corner.

CLOGHANEENA S046682 3m high west wall of tower 9.5m square. Entrance on east, latrine chute on south. Held by James, Lord Dunboyne 1640. "Demolished" by 1654.

CLOGHER S040519 Footings and a 2m high section of the 2m thick NW wall remain of probable hall-house about 21m long by 10m wide set upon on a rock outcrop.

CLOGHMARTIN S121543 16m long fragment of 1.1m thick north wall of 17th century house. 28m long west wall demolished in 1970s to make way for new bawn.

CLOHEENAFISHOGE R986200 Short low section of walling with jamb of loop alone remains of castle held in 1640 by Lord Cahir.

CLONEEN S139871 NW wall with gunloop of 6m square flanker of lost house or bawn.

CLONEYHARP S040527 SE corner with stairwell of tower of O'Dwyers of Kilnamanagh granted in the 1650s to Bartholomew ffoulke. The third storey was vaulted.

Kilcolman: plan   *Castle Park: plan*   *Castle Leiny: plan*   *Ballyartella: plan*

CLOONE S129696 Traces of former Purcell tower 8m square over walls 1.6m thick on ditched platform 33m by 36m beside old river bed near River Suir.

COOLEAGH S144460 Remains incorporated in house. A "little stump of a castle" here was held in 1650s by Florence Fenell and Walter Hackett.

CROHANE S282453 Two low defaced fragments of a circular tower rising from a base 11.7m square. The eastern fragment has part of a latrine chute. See page 173.

CORMACKSTOWN S085567 Three sides remain of hexagonal bawn 28m across with wall 0.9m thick on rock outcrop. Blocked gateway facing SW. Farm buildings to east.

CURRABAHA R981695 Footings of house 25m by 9m on moated platform 37m square.

CURRAGHMORE R985200 Just one low defaced wall 7m long with gap of former loop.

DRANGAN S283408 3m high north wall of bawn set on low crag. Minor remains of west wall. Other walls and interior platform quarried away some time in 19th century.

DRUMMIN S178712 Buried footings only of tower 13.5m by 7m. Still two storeys high with remains of upper vault in 19th century but reduced to one wall by 1902.

FENNOR S272620 North gable of castle held by Pierce Butler in 1650s near church with residential rooms over vaults at west end.

GARRYKENNEDY R768839 SW corner with second storey mural chamber on quay by Lough Derg. Belonged to Daniel O'Brien in 1640. Described in 1654-6 as "demolished".

GLASSDRUM R897475 Small low shapeless fragment of walling by roadside.

GLENAHILTY R954838 Much altered and lowered tower 10.6m by 8.8m incorporated in house. Entrance faces east. Spiral stair in SE corner blocked at bottom. See p173.

GORTACULLIN S068135 Defaced west end of tower two storeys high in farmyard.

GORTKELLY S018607 1.5m thick south wall of tower standing 3m high set upon summit 19m by 23m of revetted motte on ridge. Triangular bailey to NW.

GRAIGONE S037519 Fragments up to three storeys high of two thin walls of tower.

GRANGE R870823 9m long and 1.1m thick west wall of gatehouse stands 4m high. Central entrance passage was flanked on either side by small chambers.

GREENANE R914394 Motte only remains of castle garrisoned in the 1650s by Commonwealth troops.

INCH S052636 Motte once 6m high much damaged since 1945. No traces of stone castle built in 1303. Survey then mentions chapel, kitchen, stable, granary, kiln, etc.

INCHIROURKE S255630 Slight remains (not on map). Held by Pierce Butler in 1650s.

KILDANOGE S068134 Slight remains. Described in 1650s as "a little castle unroofed".

KILFADDA M920008 Platform bisected by lane. D-shaped tower 5.3m across with groin-vault and bawn wall stubs is now regarded as a 19th century folly or rebuild.

KILFEAKLE R958372 Motte and bailey by church with traces of small tower in ditch. Built 1192, destroyed 1196, restored in 1203. Footings of tower to north at 955385.

KILLEEN S206495 Part of 1.1m thick west wall and footings of north wall of house of Spencer family about 7m wide. Footings of part of north wall of bawn to the east.

KILMACOGUE R753651 Square platform enclosed by rampart and ditch, SW causeway.

LAHARDAN S169560 37m diameter platform with causeway on east across wet ditch. Traces of stonework footings by entrance facing causeway.

LISDALLEEN S184711 Short 3m high fragment of tower 9.2m by 7.4m. with wing facing SW. Held in 161 by Lord Ikerrin and John Purcell as trustees of William O'Meagher.

LORRHA M921045 Mound by river rising 4m to summit 10m across. Bailey to west. Destroyed by Muirchertach O'Brien in 1208 but rebuilt by Justiciar in 1221.

MAGINSTOWN S144300 Featureless fragments only of north and south walls.

MILLTOWN S058508 End wall of four storey tower 5.5m wide near river with remains of vaulting over third storey. Shown on 1840 map as wing of large building. See p153.

MYLERSTOWN S220246 Named after Milo le Poer but probably of later date. South wall only remains with one large opening at second storey level.

MULLAGHNONEY S143268 Slight traces of footings upon on rock outcrop.

OLDCASTLE S100833 Overgrown platform 24m square with retaining wall on south side (where old map shows a building) and other fragments. Ditch on west side.

OUTERAGH S076294 Fallen fragments of Butler tower possibly blown up in 1640s.

PALLAS R792789 Held by Donogh O'Brien in 1640 but ruined by 1650s. Fallen
    fragments on rock with narrow wet moat crossed by causeway on west side.
PALLAS R023637 Tower held by Walter Butler in 1641 now two storeys high and
    lacking NW end wall. Vault gone. Broken entrance on NE side. In platform 40m by 24m.
RATHNALEEN R885803 3m high fragment of tower east wall with fallen fragment and
    footings. Bank of bawn 50m square with possible gatehouse footings on north side.
SHANACLOGH R842777 Defaced NW and NE walls of building 12m by 9.4m with latrine
    turret 2.7m wide projecting 4m to NE at north corner. See page 173.
SHANBALLY S141536 Basement beside house of Cantwell tower 10.5m square. Three
    damaged loops. West wall with entrance, mural chamber & staircase mostly destroyed.
SHANCASHLAUN S113353 Overgrown multiple ditches surround bawn 50m across with
    fragments and footings on south side. An "old broken castle" in 1650.
SHANRAHAN R991135 Only two defaced fragments remain. It appears there was a
    projecting wing.
TULLAHEEDY R845778 NW corner of tower precariously standing three storeys high on
    eminence. A mullion-and-transom window facing north survived until the 19th century.
TULLAMOYLIN R879732 Footings of round-cornered tower 9.7m by 7.8m lie on low
    mound close to field with earthworks of deserted village with hut sites and sunk way.
URARD or BLACK CASTLE S289620 13m long north wall and 10.5m long west wall.
URRA R819884 Destroyed in 1985 to build a silage pit except for fragment of east wall.
Earth ramparts remain of the NE and SW corner bastions of a star-shaped fort of c1650
at Longfordpass (S239604). A contemporary battery lay upon an earlier ringwork at
Borrisnafarney (S0487546). Other earthworks not described elsewhere in the text are:
MOTTES (* with a bailey): Ballylusky R907882, Ballysheelin* S092453, Brookley or
    Drom S064687, Bruis R838331, Burgesbeg R772738, Cloncannon S037784,
    Cooloran S265268, Garranacanty* R909372, Greenane R914394, Inch 052636,
    Killanafinch R961749 & 964748, Killeen* S042045, Kilnashanally R910710,
    Lorrha M921035, Moatquarter S057824, Murgasty R884365, Rathfalla* R912792,
    Rathnaleen R892811, Rocklow S192371, Tipperary* R890370, Tullaheedy*
    R837776, Tullamain S150355
RINGWORKS: Ballynamoe S076815, Borrisnafarney
    S048756,Clareen R827781, Cookhill S045579,
    Garraun R989897, Grange S066550, Greenan
    R952656, Killamoyne R997658, Knockans
    S009755, Lisdonowley S177660, Lisduff
    S067815, Lisnageela S118853, Lisnahara
    R922723, Moycarkey S140516, Newtown
    S076525, Park S003807, Shevry R960598,
    Sopwell R964945, Summerhill M618182

CASTLE SITES IN TIPPERARY

Ballynaclough Castle

BALLINA R705732 Housing estate on site of 15th century tower on rock guarding bridge
    over Shannon. Held by Donogh O'Brien in 1640. Ruinous in 1650s.
BALLINGARRY S298487 Site of castle held by Fannings family in 17th century.
BALLINHALLA S040147 Site. Shown as moated platform 33m across on old OS map.
BALLYBOY S005142 Site of castle "covered in thatch" in the 1650s.
BALLYDAVID S183551 2.5m high remains of tower 12m by 8.7m now removed.
BALLYDREHID S037280 Site of "old broken castle" mentioned in 1650.
BALLYMURREEN S172535 House on site of castle & bawn mentioned in 1654-6 survey.
BALLYNAMOE S073816 Thinly walled late 17th century house ruin. Site of a McEgan
    castle described in the 1654-6 Civil Survey as "a stumpe of an old castle all waste".
BARONSTOWN S148654 Site of tower of the Purcells of Loughmoe on rock outcrop.
BAURSTOOKEEN S012384 Settlement earthworks are the only remains at this site.

BAWN S862755 12m length of 3.5m high bawn wall now removed.

BEAKSTOWN S092555 Ruined house on site of castle besieged by Confederate forces for a year in 1640s. Doorway reset in building shown as "Old Corn Mill" on old map.

BIRDHILL R700678 Site of castle shown on Doneley's sketches of 1681 is behind house.

BLACKCASTLE S123326 Low mound on site. Second castle nearby now vanished.

BOYTONRATH S046346 Hall-house about 16m by 10m named after Boyton family. "An old broken castle" by 1650. Last remains and earthworks have now disappeared.

BREANSHA R886331 Described as "demolished" in 1650, but ruin survived until 1840s.

BRITTAS S126615 19th century folly castle replaced bawn and buildings burnt c1820.

CARROW S828735 Site of castle said to have been destroyed c1790.

CASHLAUNCREEN R979594 Slight traces of footings despite levelling of site.

CASTLEJOHN S396321 House of Shepherd family garrisoned by Commonwealth troops during the 1650s. No remains.

CASTLE SHEPPARD R977950 18th century house in front of castle site.

CASTLETOWN R736813 Site of castle shown as ruin on 1840 Ordance Survey map.

CASTLEWALLER R759625 19th century house and bawn built from older materials.

CLOCULLY S166156 Described in 1650s as "two thatched houses with chemneyes and a bawn about them". No remains.

CLOGHINCH R955691 Site of Kennedy castle on Esker beside Nenagh River.

CLOGHONAN R945692 Site of ruin surviving in 19th century redeveloped for house.

CLOGHPRIOR R859891 House on or near site of castle marked on old OS map.

CLONCANNON S030774 Moated platform by Ollatrim River possibly site of "castle wanting repaire and a mill seated upon a brooke" mentioned in 1654-6 Civil Survey.

CLONISMULLEN S058682 Site of castle held by John Stapleton in 1640.

CORDANGAN R905330 Site of castle which was "irrepayreable" in the 1650s.

CRANNA R786727 House on site of castle "out of repayre" in 1650s.

DERRYLEIGH R739615 Castle "ruines" with "barbican" in 1654-6 removed c1839.

DRANGAN S019307 Site of "demolished burnt castle" mentioned in 1650s.

DRUMLUMMIN R988164 Remains of castle of barons of Cahir levelled in 1950s. Mid 17th century house site to west excavated in 1981.

DOUGHKILL N017012 Remains of tower 7.2m square over walls 1.4m thick with circular SE corner turret removed to enable widening of road in 1973.

DUNALLEY R828710 Quarrying has removed remains of tower 9m by 6m with traces of spiral stair in SE corner. Held by John Kennedy 1640. Had a "barbican" in 1654-6.

DUNDRUM R981448 Site of chief seat of O'Dwyer family. Described in 1650s as a castle with a large bawn.

FERTIANA S095546 Remains of tower stood 3m high until early 20th century. Held by Theobald Purcell in 1640. Described 1654 as a "stump of a castle...out of repair".

FISHMOYNE S050672 19th century house probably lies on site of castle already very ruined by the 1650s.

FORGESTOWN S131516 6.7m long east wall demolished in 1980s. Barn & yard on site. Said to have had vaults over second and fourth of five levels and two bartizans.

FREMANS S105136 Site of castle and bawn mentioned in the 1650s.

GARRANLEA S051333 Site of castle and bawn mentioned in 1650s.

GARRAUN S132438 Rubble mound now gone. Sold by John Hacket in early 17th century to Walter Sall.

GLENBEHA S123851 8m long, 2m high length of wall 2m thick survived until recently.

GRANGE S063552 Ditched platform 20m square. L-plan building on old map now gone.

GRENANSTOWN R944760 House formerly dated 1695 on site of castle held by John Grace in 1640, materials from which were reused.

KILCARREN M942027 Farmyard of house on site of circular tower.

KILKNOCKAN S209371 Slight traces of earthworks are only remains.

KILLERK S195325 Site of "old broken castle mentioned in 1650s.

KILLINANE S105597 Crucifix on platform in graveyard is supposed site of castle destroyed by a hurricane in 1838.

KNOCKANROE S134774 Approximate site of ruin shown on 1840 map, gone by 1904.
LAFFALY R937339 Site of castle "wanting repayre" in 1650.
LAGGANSTOWN S024348 Site of castle of the earls of Ormond.
LISHEEN S170671 11m high NE corner with walls 2m high still stood in 19th century.
LISSANISKY R938790 18th century house on site of castle occupied by Daniel O'Meara
    in 1640 but described as "demolished castle with a slate house adioyneing" in 1654-6.
LISSAVA S041249 Site of castle reduced to a "stump" by the 1650s.
MELDRUM S119416 Slight traces of earthworks south of castle site. Stone dated 1622
    with initials of G.Meldrum and D.Sall now at Meldrum House.
MERTONHALL R931898 Site of "old bawne" mentioned in Civil Survey of 1654-6.
MILLBROOK R921735 Old stonework and timbers reused in ruined house & outbuildings.
MOCKLERSTOWN S159312 Site of castle and bawn mentioned in 1650.
MODREENY R956899 Fallen fragments now part of rockery in garden of later house.
    Held by John Carroll in 1641. Described as "old castle and bawne" in 1654-6.
MONAQUILL R902722 19th century house on site of castle or 30m east of it.
MONROE R802818 Wall 7m long and 2m thick remained in 19th century.
OLDCASTLE R575487 O'Dwyer castle. A "stump" by 1654. Rubble pile by 1840
OLDCASTLE S088711 Traces of castle granted in 1612 to John Cantwell survived until
    mid 20th century.
PALLAS M998070 Farmyard on site of bawn with 1.1m thick wall still 3.5m high in 19th
    century. Described in 1654 as "old irrepayarable castle and bawn".
PARKMORE S131880 Approximate location of castle mentioned in 1654-6 survey.
PARKSTOWN S157517 House or outbuildings may incorporate old masonry or materials.
RAPLA R887826 Circular hilltop site 48m by 56m. Castle gone but ice-house remains.
RATHRONAN S206259 Site of burnt-out shell of castle held by Brookes family in 1650.
REDMONDSTON S241251 Slight traces only of castle probably held by Le Poers.
REHILL R974188 Site of castle and bawn held in 1640 by Lord Cahir.
RICHMOND R846810 Ruined late 18th century house reuses older materials.
ROCKFOREST S204862 Site only of Maghers' tower of Knockballymagher, 17th century
    house with round stair turret, and James Hutchinson's house of c1712.
RORARDSTOWN S079658 Site of castle held by Phillip Purcell in 1640.
ROSSESTOWN S139621 Platform may be site of castle held in 1640 by John Purcell and
    William Prendergast. A bawn is also mentioned in the Cil Survey of 1654-6.
SLEVOIR M873015 Held by James Butler in 1640 but "wholly demolished" by 1654-6.
SHANNONHALL R805838 Site levelled & robbed. Door jamb moved to garden of house.
SOLLOGHODBEG R890400 Described in 1650s as "irepayrable"..."a stump". Gone.
TOMONA R795839 Modern house on site of castle already ruinous in the 1650s.
TULLAMAIN S151352 House of 1835-8 on probable site of stone castle. A motte and
    bailey lie in trees to the NW.
OTHER CASTLE SITES: Ballinlonty S061656, Ballycarron S003337, Ballygibbon
    R929835, Ballygown R832729, Ballykerin S281475, Ballynacourty R858294,
    Ballymore S021465, Black Castle S076576, Carrigeensharragh S219288, Castle
    Loaghny R795389, Cathaganstown S196441, Curragh S097130, Donaskeagh
    R956419, Dromline R939356, Garrangibbon S355304 Graigue S127668,
    Graiguepadeeen S252617, Greyfort R926936, Harley Park S363459, Kilmoyler
    S016299, Knockane R993193, Knockuragh S284408, Lyonstown S107366,
    Poyntztown S253524, Rahinane R974966, Rathcool S519371, Rodeen R875915,
    Rathduff R815402, Uskane R945963, Woodinstown S100309
POSSIBLE CASTLE SITES: Ballybeg S137170, Ballyboe S246264, Ballydine S331232,
    Ballynacroe S791368, Ballynilard R867352, Boolaglass R776791, Carrigeen S081344,
    Clonacody S212316, Clonbrick S857441, Emly R767347, Grangemore S109457,
    Kilboy R863719, Knockeevan S172286, Knockloft S143198, Lismacue R966328,
    Mertonhall R931898, Mobarnan S168399, Mohober S346457, Near S166454,
    Newpark S118442, Noan S166454, Orchardstown S191272, Sadleirswells R984376,
    Windmill S068388.

FURTHER READING

Castles in Ireland, Tom McNeill, 1997
The Architecture of Ireland, Maurice Craig, 1982
The Medieval Castles of Ireland, David Sweetman, 1999
Medieval Ireland, An Archaeology, Tadhg O'Keeffe, 2000
Irish Castles and Castellated Houses, 1941, Harold Leask
Archaeological Inventory of County Tipperary, Duchas, 2002
Guide to the National Monuments of Ireland, Peter Harbison, 1970
The Shell Guide to Ireland, Lord Killanin and Michael Duignan, 1969

Garrykennedy: plan

See the series of articles by Richard Cronin, Martin Breen and others in The Other Clare. This source contains extra historical material for Clare Castles and additional plans of Cratloemore, Donogrogue, Ennis, Ennistymon, Glencolumbkille, Gragan and Lissylisheen.
See also the annual journals of the Royal Irish Academy, the Royal Society of Antiquaries of Ireland and various other archaeological and historical societies throughout Ireland.
Guide pamphlets or leaflets are available for Bunratty, Craggaunowen, Cahir, Carrick-on-Suir, Limerick, and Roscrea.

A GLOSSARY OF TERMS

BAILEY - Defensible space enclosed by a wall or a palisade and ditch. BARTIZAN - Turret corbelled out from a corner. BAWN - A walled enclosure. CORBEL - A projecting bracket supporting other stonework or timber beams. HALL-HOUSE - A two storey building containing a hall or chamber over a basement. HOODMOULD - Projecting moulding above an arch or lintel to throw off water. JAMB - The side of a doorway, window or other opening. JOGGLED-LINTEL - Lintel of several pieces with zig-zag joints to prevent slipping. KEEP - A citadel or final strongpoint. In the medieval period such buildings were called donjons. LIGHT - A compartment of a window. LINTEL - A stone or beam spanning an opening. LOOP - A small opening to admit light or for the discharge of missiles. MACHICOLATION - A slot for dropping or shooting missiles at assailants. MOAT - A ditch, water filled or dry, around an enclosure. MOTTE - Partly or wholly man-made castle mound. MULLION - A vertical member dividing the lights of a window. MURDER-HOLE - An internal machicolation, often in the ceiling of a an entrance lobby. OGIVAL-ARCH - Arch of oriental origin with both convex and concave curves. PARAPET - A wall for protection at any sudden drop. PLINTH - The projecting base of a wall. PORTCULLIS - Wooden gate (usually iron-reinforced), designed to rise and fall in vertical grooves, being hoisted up by a windlass. RINGWORK - Enclosure of modest size defended by a high rampart. SHEELA-NA-GIG - Female fertility image with the genitals displayed. SPANDREL - A surface between an arch and the rectangle containing it. STRONGHOUSE - A mansion capable of being defended against an attack. TOWER HOUSE - self-contained house with the main rooms stacked vertically. TRACERY - Intersecting ribwork in the upper part of a Gothic window. TRANSOM - A horizontal member dividing the lights of a window. WALL-WALK - A walkway protected by a parapet on top of a wall.

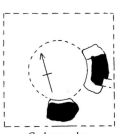
Crohane: plan

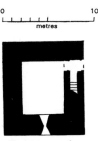
Grantstown: plan

0   10
metres

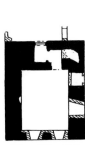
Glenahilty: plan

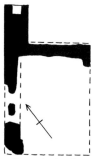
Shanaclogh: plan

INDEX OF CASTLES OF NORTH MUNSTER

FOLLY PUBLICATIONS BOOKS by Mike Salter

Folly Cottage, 151 West Malvern Rd, Malvern, Worcs WR14 4AY, England

IRISH CASTLES TITLES - Five volumes covering all of Ireland
CONNACHT   2004   104 pages, 365 illustrations
ULSTER   2004   72 pages, 200 illustrations
SOUTH MUNSTER 2004   128 pages, 340 illustrations
LEINSTER 2004 200 pages, 640 illustrations
NORTH MUNSTER 2004 176 pages, 570 illustrations

SCOTTISH CASTLES TITLES - Five volumes covering all of Scotland
SOUTH WEST SCOTLAND 1993   152 pages, 347 illustrations.
HEARTLAND OF SCOTLAND 1994 140 pages, 299 illustrations.
LOTHIAN AND BORDERS 1994 168 pages, 338 illustrations.
GRAMPIAN AND ANGUS 1995 200 pages, 370 illustrations.
WESTERN AND NORTHERN SCOTLAND 1995 152 pages, 200 illustrations.

WELSH CASTLES TITLES - Four volumes covering all of Wales
GWENT, GLAMORGAN & GOWER 2003 edition 112 pages, 250 illustrations
MID WALES 2001 edition 72 pages, 95 illustrations.
SOUTH-WEST WALES 1996 88 pages, 130 illustrations.
NORTH WALES 1997 88 pages, 125 illustrations.

ENGLISH CASTLES TITLES - Eighteen volume set, plus separate index volume
SHROPSHIRE 2001 edition 88 pages, 146 illustrations.
STAFFORDSHIRE 1997 edition 64 pages, 85 illustrations.
WARWICKSHIRE 1992 56 pages, 87 illustrations.
HEREFORDSHIRE & WORCESTERSHIRE 2000 edition 88 pages, 120 illustrations
NORTHUMBERLAND 1997 1997 120 pages, 210 illustrations.
CUMBRIA 1998 104 pages, 210 illustrations.
DEVON & CORNWALL 1999 88 pages, 146 illustrations.
SUSSEX 2000 72 pages, 100 illustrations.
KENT 2000 88 pages, 120 illustrations.
EAST ANGLIA 2001 88 pages, 130 illustrations.
SURREY 2001 24 pages, 32 illustrations.
YORKSHIRE 2001 120 pages, 215 illustrations.
LANCASHIRE & CHESHIRE 2001 40 pages, 60 illustrations.
WESSEX 2002 104 pages, 180 illustrations.
GLOUCESTERSHIRE & BRISTOL 2002 40 pages, 57 illustrations.
DURHAM 2002 64 pages, 100 illustrations.
EAST MIDLANDS 2002 100 pages, 160 illustrations.
THAMES VALLEY & THE CHILTERNS 2002 80 pages, 118 illustrations.

Also available in a similar format are books about medieval parish churches in:
Scotland (single volume), Wales (4 volumes), England (14 volumes for various counties).
Books about the Isle of Man and the Channel Islands cover both castles and churches.

A supplement with extra plans and photos of Irish Castles not included in the books is available free to any customers ordering books direct from the author-publisher.

WEB SITE   www.follypublications.co.uk

Gives details of prices, forthcoming titles, news and views, and how to order books.